Library of
Davidson College

Poems of R. P. Blackmur

Poems of R. P. Blackmur

with introduction by Denis Donoghue

Princeton University Press, Princeton, New Jersey

Copyright © 1977 by Princeton University Press
Published by Princeton University Press, Princeton, New Jersey.
In the United Kingdom: Princeton University Press, Guildford, Surrey

ALL RIGHTS RESERVED

Library of Congress Cataloging in Publication Data will
be found on the last printed page of this book
Publication of this book has been aided by the Paul Mellon Fund of
Princeton University Press
This book has been composed in Linotype Electra
Printed in the United States of America
by Princeton University Press, Princeton, New Jersey

Contents

Introduction by Denis Donoghue   ix

FROM JORDAN'S DELIGHT, 1937

From Jordan's Delight	3
Of Lucifer	13
An Elegy for Five	16
For Horace Hall	19
Sea Island Miscellany	21
Judas Priest	29
Views of Boston Common and Near By	31
Witness of Light	33
October Frost	34
Steriles Ritournelles	35
Petit Manan Point	36
Three Songs at Equinox	38
The Cough	40
Phasellus Ille	43
Scarabs for the Living	44
Since There's No Help . . .	50
Simulacrum Deae	51
Pone Metum . . .	52
River-Walk	53
Dedications	55
A Labyrinth of Being	59
A Funeral for a Few Sticks	65

THE SECOND WORLD, 1942

The Second World	73
Missa Vocis	74
Una Vita Nuova	75
For Comfort and for Size	76

Rats, Lice, and History	77
Before Sentence Is Passed	79
The Cellar Goes Down with a Step	85
The Idea of Christian Society	86
The Dead Ride Fast	87

THE GOOD EUROPEAN, 1947

Twelve Scarabs for the Living: 1942	91
Three Poems from a Text: Isaiah LXI:1-3	95
Thirteen Scarabs for the Living: 1945	99
The Good European: 1945	
I. A Decent Christian Burial	103
II. Phoenix at Loss	106
III. Dinner for All	107
IV. Coda: Respublica Christiana	109
Sunt Lacrimae Rerum et Mentem Mortalia Tangunt	110
Boy and Man: The Cracking Glass	111
Miching Mallecho	112
The Rape of Europa	113
Ithyphallics	114
The Communiqués from Yalta	115

PREVIOUSLY UNCOLLECTED POEMS

Autumn Sonata: To John Marshall	119
A Testament on Faith	124
Mr. Virtue and the Three Bears	130
Alma Venus	132
Last Things	134
Effigy	135
Three Poems	
Water-Ruined	137
Flower and Weed	137
Of a Muchness	138
Ides of March to April Fool's	139
Night Piece	143

Less Love Than Eachness	144
Resurrection	145
The Bull	146
By Definition	147
On Excited Knees	148
Half-Tide Ledge	149
All's the Foul Fiend's	150
Nigger Jim	151
And No Amends	152
Threnos	153
Acknowledgments	154

R. P. Blackmur's Poetry: An Introduction
by Denis Donoghue

It is commonly assumed that Richard Blackmur (1904-1965) was a critic by nature and a poet only betimes; a professor in one capacity and, in the other, an amateur, almost a gentleman. The relation between the poetry and the criticism has not been examined. The criticism, taken by itself, has always been in dispute but never in doubt. *Language as Gesture* and *The Lion and the Honeycomb* are discussed by nearly everyone who thinks that criticism matters. Some readers find the books exasperating, their insights wild, bizarre, wilful in style; and there are readers who blame Henry James for giving Blackmur, when he was a promising young man, the stylistic procedures of *The Golden Bowl* instead of sober counsel. Other readers revel in the books, yielding themselves to the swoon of apprehension: they take the critical essays as the next best thing to Longinus on the Sublime, and they wait for the blow and shock of perception as if nothing else mattered. Blackmur named Aristotle and Coleridge as his masters in criticism, and labored under their joint auspices, but the testament is not convincing: in critical practice he was a sublimist at heart, attending upon the circumstance of literature only for the thrill of seeing circumstance transcended, conditions refuted by a stroke of the poet's imagination beyond every prediction. He was interested in explanations, subject to the qualification that he thought them ultimately beside the point. When Ophelia says, "To have seen what I have seen, see what I see," there is little point in offering explanations based upon the chain of being, the structure of Elizabethan parliaments, the hermetic tradition, theatres indoor and outdoor, and so forth. We sway with the rhythm of feeling, or we withhold ourselves: there is no other choice. The imagination is the ordinary mind in an extraordinary phase, far beyond its predicted course. The conditions imposed upon the imagination are important and at certain times may be nearly fatal; this is the desperate theme of *The Lion and the Honeycomb* and *Anni Mirabiles*, the latter especially a heart-rending and almost heartbroken meditation on the circumstances in which the modern poetic imagination has been compelled to live. If Blackmur's critical heart did not break in fact, the reason is that he came upon examples of the imagination exulting, or seeming to exult, in circumstances which should have made it impossible for it to work at all. The imagination always plays against the odds: in criticism, the odds are reckoned, described, mulled over. Brooding upon the conditions in which the imagination is forced to live is itself a poetic act, and it is an open question in the twentieth century whether the brooding is likelier to issue in a poem or an essay: the difference, so far as the quick of perception goes, is not absolute. Some writers write poems and then surround the poetry with prose for warmth, sustenance, good company: readers are eased into the verse or incited to rise to its occasion. Eliot, Pound, Yeats, Stevens, Williams are cases in this point; poets first and always, prose-men on occasion and for marginal reasons. In some writers the poems are the main thing, but hard work, too hard to practice as a daily trade and therefore enforced as a Lenten exercise. I think of the poets Ransom and Empson in this way: in each, the criticism gives an air of leisure, cultivated ease, the mind engaged with congenial materials but patient, speculative, unharassed. In a third and, for the moment, final class there are writers in whom the occasions roughly labeled "creative" and "critical" join to provoke a third person, the man of letters: a person literary through and through but unsystematic in the form of his perceptions. Sometimes the perceptions urge upon the writer a special vocation of form, perhaps a fiction, a set of rival attitudes implying a possible novel; or they let him take their force by themes, consecutively, as in sentences, paragraphs, essays. In this class I think of Trilling, Burke, Winters, Tate, Richards, Wilson, and Blackmur. Of these men, these third persons, it is reasonable to say that no single work gives their gist. Each essay, poem, or fiction is merely one part of an enterprise which cannot expect to find itself completed at all. An essay or a poem by Blackmur is a glancing blow of the mind, provisional, *ad hoc* or *ad rem*, but never adequate as an epitome, the entire life of his mind in little. I am not referring to the merely technical fact that several of his projects remained in an unfinished state: from time to time we heard of major books, works in progress on Dostoevsky, James, Henry Adams which never progressed beyond a few capital chapters. I refer to the fact, not at all technical, that we have to sense the life of Blackmur's mind by adding piece to piece and allowing the force of each to become, as it will, implicative: the unity of his mind is what we aspire to feel, not something given to us in samples. This makes a problem for the anthologist. I have sometimes thought of assembling a *Portable Blackmur*, but the thought is useless, his mind does not offer itself in summary, sample, or gist. In one of his moods he could be as direct as any other critic; aphoristic, if the mood were extreme. There are sentences which a student might transfer to his commonplace book without further ado. But in other moods, and those more frequent than the first, Blackmur had to woo and caress the sentences before they would respond to his perception, and normally the perception was lost or abandoned if it were taken away from its atmosphere and deprived it of its aura. Some readers are impatient with Blackmur in this character; they think of his essays as failed poems, a menace in prose if a caress by intention. Criticism is supposed to be prosaic: mandarins are suspect. But the truth is that Blackmur's prose is never (well, rarely, then, if we must be strict) self-indulgent. He is registering experiences exceptional in their delicacy and strength: he does not believe that there are words for everything or that the standard words in standard sequences will answer every need. I have never understood why the impatient readers do not give Blackmur the benefit of the doubt, when there is doubt or suspicion; why they do not wait and see whether or not his seemingly far-fetched paragraphs are worth the carriage. Let me mention a case in point. *Anni Mirabiles* is the text of four lectures given at the Library of Congress in 1956. The lectures must have been difficult to listen to: immensely complex, elaborately organized in themes, images, allusions. On the printed page the difficulties are eased, but the reader must still take them slowly, letting them invade his mind, engaging Blackmur's passion with a response at least similar in kind. I speak personally at this point. I cannot think of any other book which speaks of modern literature with such understanding, such intimacy. It is not merely a work of mind; or at least the description is helpless unless we think of mind as consciousness, conscience, vitality, the whole nervous system brought into play upon the crucial issues. I speak of issues, not themes: the issues are absolutely central to our sense of the imagination and the public conditions it encounters; the new illiteracy of partial and specialized knowledge; the malicious criticism of genuine knowledge; expressionism; bourgeois humanism and the secular forms of imagination; all the techniques of trouble, and the predicament of the artist as he falls into further trouble and flounders between spontaneity and achieved form.

Blackmur came upon these predicaments early and responded to them, within the limits of his vision, in verse and prose: if the later prose is more ambitious than the earlier work, it is because he confronted the public forces more and more directly and was less and less content to take them silently and for granted. In the early criticism he felt that ideas and attitudes became matters of critical concern only so far as they transpired in word, cadence, rhythm, in the poem itself: he wanted not the idea but its technical pressure or form. In the later criticism he spoke of ideas and attitudes directly, whether they transpired in the poetry or not. Naturally, the European novel rather than the English or American poem allowed for this procedure: when you are commenting upon *Anna Karenina*, especially if you are already compromising the occasion by dealing with an English translation, you are inclined to take a further license in treating its constituents somewhat expansively. Purity of texture in the fiction is already a lost cause. From verse to the novel; there is a corresponding movement from the personal themes of Blackmur's first book of poetry, *From Jordan's Delight* (1937) to the social and public themes of the later poems in *The Second World* (1942) and *The Good European* (1947). The direction may be verified by recourse to the volumes of criticism: *The Double Agent* (1935), *The Expense of Greatness* (1940), *Language as Gesture* (1952), *The Lion and the Honeycomb* (1955), *Eleven Essays in the European Novel* (1964), and the last gathering of prose, *A Primer of Ignorance* (1967), edited by Blackmur's friend and colleague Joseph Frank.

It is probably wise to approach the poems by admitting that they have not, or at least not yet, established themselves as exerting much pressure upon contemporary poetry. "The waste remains, the waste remains and kills." Blackmur was inspiring to several poets as a presence, an example of intelligence at work in language, but it was mostly for his personal sake or for things he wrote as a critic. He is present in at least three of John Berryman's *Dream Songs* (173, 210, and 282). "Mr. Blackmur, which are the holy cities of America?" someone in England is reported as having asked the famous cirtic; an episode that lodged in Berryman's mind as significant of something or other and worth putting in verse. In Robert Lowell's poem "Playing Ball with the Critic" the critic is Blackmur, indelibly present in Lowell's mind for having said in a review of his early poems: "[Mr. Lowell] does not seem to have decided whether his Roman Catholic belief is the form of a force or the sentiment of a form. . . . As it is now, logic lacerates the vision and vision turns logic to zealotry." For all I know, there may be many other poets who carry around in their minds Blackmurian notations which have entered their poems, acknowledged or not. But the fact of waste remains: Blackmur's poems are not invoked as readily as his criticism or his personality.

There is waste, even in circumstances which should make for a choice communication. Think of Blackmur, to recite an instance of waste, in relation to one reader, Wallace Stevens. Here are the facts. Blackmur was an early and appreciative critic of Stevens' poems: the evidence comes in several essays. Stevens remarked that he never read critiques of his own work, but "never" is a big word: he meant "rarely" and made an exception in Blackmur's favor. Stevens and Blackmur were not close friends, hardly friends at all but civilized acquaintances: they did not really hit it off. On May 14, 1942, Stevens wrote to the Cummington Press asking them to send along a copy of Blackmur's book of poems, *The Second World*, which Cummington had just published. When it arrived, he showed no interest in the poems, but only in the book as an object, its format, binding, and color, and found none of these attributes to his liking. Cummington was about to publish Stevens' *Notes Toward a Supreme Fiction*, and he spoke up in favor of light colors for the cover in linen or buckram. Katharine Frazier of the Cummington Press mentioned a technical problem in regard to one of Blackmur's lines. Stevens took the matter up, but only to say that the line was "an unusually full one," meaning unusually long by comparison with his own. It would be pleasant to think that Stevens was interested in Blackmur's book as a collection of poems, a work of imagination, but it is impossible. One of Blackmur's poorest poems, "Rats, Lice, and

History," caught Stevens' attention when he came across it in *The Nation*, but only because he approved of its general contempt for politicians. Blackmur's prose, too, Stevens thought pretentious, making too much ado. But at least he offered a dazzling reason for not admiring his work. When Blackmur published "Notes on Eleven Poets," in the *Kenyon Review* (Spring 1945), Stevens mentioned the review to Henry Church, saying that "as an expositor of ideas Blackmur fails, not for lack of ideas, but for not knowing what his ideas are." One usually comes away from reading ten or twelve pages of his work, Stevens said, "longing for sex and politics." As a matter of fact, Blackmur's poems have plenty of sex and politics: for my taste and interest, too much of the latter and just the right amount of the former. The politics goes better in Blackmur's prose, the sex in the verse. But the point is simple: that Stevens felt himself temperamentally alien to Blackmur, though Blackmur did not feel himself alien to Stevens. There is a great deal more poetry and more imagination in Blackmur's poems than Stevens was willing to recognize. My guess is that Stevens, who always knew what his own ideas were, was sullen toward Blackmur's verse because it maintained as a problem rather than as a discovery the relation between idea and image. But there is little point in guessing.

Stevens could not have faulted Blackmur's themes; many of them are perennial like his own, the great abstractions which, to begin with, are hardly more than projects for poetry. The poems speak of loneliness, love, death, "the nightmare, If," desire, loss, "our inward beggary," terror, war, the question of sense and faith, the twist of chaos and order, the torsions of experience. As a Maine man, Blackmur turned to the sea for images of a continuity relished or feared; but those, too, are common enough. A more characteristic theme of Blackmur's is what a poem in *The Good European* calls "the shambles under the human mind," a quirky preoccupation in prose and verse. Like Stevens, Blackmur revered the mind, but he had his own special sense of the relation between mind and shambles. Many of Stevens' poems may be described as making a music of thought, showing the mind moving, turning back upon itself, charting the possible ways of seeing things. Chaos is felt as offering a problem of method rather than as a force incorrigible in its humiliation of every method. Blackmur loved thought, but he felt that it was nearly always premature. He valued thinking rather than thought, because thinking never forgets that it is a process rather than a doctrine: thought is the mind already too much made up, congealed in conclusions. He wanted mind to regard itself as a form of feeling, or a relatively early phase in the history of its feeling; so that its discoveries would be kept fresh and scrupulous. The shambles under the mind offered a desperate situation, but at least kept the mind in a state of humility and perhaps of grace. What then of conviction, belief, principle, and knowledge itself? In *Anni Mirabiles* and elsewhere Blackmur deplored the malicious criticism of knowledge which accounted for much of modern philosophy and drove intelligence into the sand; but he did not contradict himself, the only conviction worth having was forced upon a man by a blow of experience, the only belief worth holding was inseparable from unbelief, the best principles were forced upon an honest man not as programs but as hunches, gravities, decencies. As for knowledge, it was genuine when animated by a sense of everything that lay beneath it or ranged beyond it; elusive in both capacities. What Blackmur valued, then, was the apprehensive character of mind. Many of his poems are strategies to keep the mind from becoming too fixed in its habits.

So with words. One of Blackmur's favorite citations was a sentence from Elizabeth Sewell's little monograph on Valéry: "Words are the mind's one defense against possession by thought or dreams; even Jacob kept trying to find out the name of the angel he wrestled with." Blackmur liked the sentence so much that he assumed he always quoted it accurately: not so, it often came out a little wrong as "words are the only defense of the mind against being possessed by thought or dream." But no matter; in either version it offered a justification of words, a critique of authoritarian thought, and an account of where dreams belonged. Blackmur loved every attribute of words except their fixity, and he took the harm out of fixity by giving words their head, not frivolously but experimentally. On the first page of *From Jordan's Delight* the language is encouraged to run from "boy" to "buoy" to "buoyed." Later there is serious play with "spend," "spendthrift," "spent," "unspent." It is not that Blackmur thought language wiser than any poet, but it is better in one respect, the mobility of its relations: words do not make up their minds in advance or settle prematurely upon limits. Let me revise something I have just now said. Blackmur loved words, but he loved even more the process that led to words: "chance flowering to choice," when the choice words turn out right. In "The Journeyman Rejoices," in *From Jordan's Delight*, Blackmur speaks of

> some bleak and gallant face,
> Lonely in words, but under words at home.

Later in the book he invokes "the crying out that echoes solitude," and later still

> the wordless and unsummoned sense that springs
> indifferent beneath all words?

and there is a phrase far out in the book about unhappy ripeness reaching

> from heart to groin to word
> drenching each with each.

Let these move through the poetry as mottoes, as if to say that Blackmur in loving the craft of words loved the unconscious skills and needs and cries which find in words, sometimes when luck holds, their appeasement. In *The Second World*

> One tries at last
> to say only what the heart says, do only
> what the buds do: flower by conviction:
> the inward mastery of the outward act.

It is wonderful to act upon whim and then find the whim endorsed by reason.

We often assume of poets enamored of words that they are enslaved to the sounds, the lullings and the relishes of language. They are poets more of ear than of eye. This does not necessarily mean that they are drunk with words and gone beyond the sobriety of caring what the words mean. More often than not, it means that the poet chooses among meanings those that emerge from the phonetic relations of words; a different matter, and not at all a disgrace. Blackmur more often refers to "the inward ear" and "the mind's ear" than to "the mind's eye," and he more often judges situations according to the propriety of words spoken in them than of words offered to delineate them. The propriety of the words spoken seems to reveal the grace of the relation from which they have emerged; as in 'The Cough' She says to Him

> —Words verge on flesh, and so we may,
> someday, be to ourselves the things we say.

(But I concede that the poem gives Him the last word, appealing beyond "your mere word" to "the still body.") And since we are speaking of the propriety of words, we must advert to whatever comes before the words, the quality of the silence which incites them. One of Blackmur's "Scarabs for the Living" reads thus:

> Quiet the self, and silence brims like spring:
> the soaking in of light, the gathering
> of shadow up, after each passing cloud,
> the green life eating into death aloud,
> the hum of seasons; all on beating wing.

The hum of seasons becomes, in the verse, the hum and buzz of implication; not merely sensory images but what the images have become as experiences along with other experiences not necessarily sensory at all. We are instructed to say, these days, that the relation between nature and culture has been naively represented; that, in fact, virtually nothing is nature, virtually everything culture. Let it be so. Then Blackmur's scarab has to do with the ways in which individual experience, an affair of culture through and through if you will, is amplified and enriched by forces which he calls (since their fulfilment is words) silence. "Words are the mind's one defense. . . ." I take Elizabeth Sewell's sentence to mean that the humanity of a mind possessed by dreams is in abeyance, the rift between its subconscious and its conscious life is abysmal; when possessed by thought, the same mind is congealed, transfixed by its mere contents. Either way, the true, continuous life of feeling is suppressed. Words release the human sound again by giving the mind not an official syntax but its possibility, the constituents of feeling and speech. Blackmur was not obsessed or even bemused by words; he turned to words for protection against every kind of obsession to which the mind is tempted, since words contain the experience of others as well as our own. Language is therefore to Blackmur "the country of the blue," a phrase from James' story "The Next Time" that lived in Blackmur's mind as a motif and a motive. In the third of "Three Poems from a Text" certain memories are said to be

> of the country of the blue, too far
> for capture and too near to see at once.

Blackmur thought of the country of the blue, the place which in James's story houses the artist with "a good conscience and a great idea," as "a very lonely place to be, for it is very nearly empty except for the self, and is gained only by something like a religious retreat, by an approximation of birth or death or birth-in-death." These are his terms in A *Primer of Ignorance*, but as his brooding over blueness proceeds he takes the harm out of its loneliness by making it a constituent of the work of art. The artist as a mere person is lonely: "the man fully an artist is the man, short of the saint, most wholly deprived." But the loneliness is transfigured when the artist realizes that "all the professions possible in life are mutually inclusive," that "one's own profession is but the looking-glass and the image of the others." The artist is the one who "being by nature best fitted to see the image clear is damned only if he does not." If he sees it, "his vision disappears in his work, which is the country of the blue." Let us say, then, that the country of the blue is the work of art, so far as it is an achievement of the imagination, and take for granted that the artist so far as he is a man is lonely and deprived: his art makes "the great good place," or comes upon it if the art seems natural as well. I assume that memories, to return to Blackmur's poem, are of the country of the blue, but not in it, because of the difference between memory and imagination. Only a great imagination occupies the country of the blue, and even then only on occasion and with luck. Memory knows the country but knows it as "too far for capture and too near to see at once." I have said that to Blackmur the country of the blue was Language. My authority for saying it is chiefly James' story. Blackmur's commentary upon James' story would authorize a somewhat different emphasis: if the country of the blue is the achieved work of art, it is Language only at the point and in the place where it has achieved its vocation of form. The Oxford English Dictionary is not the country of the blue.

The Tempest is. The dictionary houses the words, but it does not provide vision or syntax, which are prerogatives of imagination. Language, to Blackmur, meant the possibility of a poem: words were meanings, but also provocations, hints, invitations.

Therefore he had favorite words, like favorite people. Mostly they are drawn from the language of natural description but used then as offering moral analogies. Silence "brims" like spring. The "radiance of wordless intimacies" between two people "brims to the flood." In "River-Walk" a friend is "friend of brimming silence." Feeling is associated with the welling-up of energy, nature offering culture a thousand good examples. "Vertigo" is used in several poems where the theme is reason in madness, matter and impertinency desperately mixed, a theme close to Blackmur's heart. Short of taking a word-count, I cannot prove that Blackmur's favorite word is "weather," but I will risk the assertion. As noun and verb it is diversely used to mean the following, and more besides: the nature of things ("weather is all"): weather as a stone weathers, or a landscape, or a house: profusion of feeling, as in "the drunken weather of the headlong heart": the hurly-burly of circumstance, time, change: weather as one weathers out a storm: and weather as a genial law of nature, a sustaining principle, a living culture, true *societas*:

> No order ripens into weather
> unless it bind and loose together
> chaos of good consuming ill,
> of lovers who search and shun God's will.

There is a famous essay in *Language as Gesture* in which Blackmur rebukes E. E. Cummings for using the word "flower" as a maid of all work. "The word has become an idea, and in the process has been deprived of its history, its qualities, and its meaning": a rebuke repeated in *Anni Mirabiles*, where Blackmur alleges that Cummings "deprives many of his words of as much as possible of *their own* meaning: so that they may take on *his* meaning." These strictures depend upon Blackmur's belief that "when a word is used in a poem it should be the sum of all its appropriate history made concrete and particular in the individual context; and in poetry all words act *as if* they were so used, because the only kind of meaning poetry can have requires that all its words resume their full life: the full life being modified and made unique by the qualifications the words perform one upon the other in the poem." I think this principle is fulfilled, on the whole, in Blackmur's poetry. The meaning of the word "weather" is explored, revealed, its weight and density assessed; it is not used as a blank cheque, the amount to be filled in by the reader according to whim or the looseness of his emotion. "No order ripens into weather. . . ." Presumably unripe order is order prematurely arrived at and therefore insecure and therefore assertive, rigid, a formula rather than a form. What order ripens into, if it ripens, is a theoretic form for our behavior. I use Blackmur's phrases and recall his saying that "no order remains vital which has lost its intimate contact, at some point, with the disorder or the unknown order which gave it rise." It may be said that "weather" is hard-pressed to register so much, if we agree upon the meaning in these terms, but I think it passes the test. If the ripeness is all, it is because it retains a sense of the origin of order in disorders and unknown orders. "Our great delight," Blackmur says, "is when we have transformed our aspirations into behavior." Weather is that kind of behavior, order remembering its origin, and therefore bending to the rhythm of change; but bending is not breaking, and the changes are seasonal. It is by an extension of this meaning that we come upon the last of Blackmur's favorite words in a short list: eddy, eddying, and so forth. This poet is always suspicious of forces which are content with themselves, he loves to discover a misgiving, a doubt whirling within a faith to keep the faith decent. Eddy is the word he uses to mean one's strength directed against oneself:

> There in the blossoming of waywardness,
> O stalwart Lear, you eddy and confess.

—or the personal need or quirk turned against its element

> There is no shelter here, no self-warm lair,
> When every lung eddies the ocean air.

—or energy whirling off from its congenial form ("O eddying, bodiless faith") or hanging back from its fate—

> It is the coward in me will not rest,
> but eddying against the coming time
> exhausts the prayer for safety dime by dime.

—or the politics of inertia in which not even the inertia is believed in and one is identified as an eddying standstill, as in "The Dead Ride Fast." The language of eddying is natural to Blackmur's poetry, and it is no harm at all if we think he resorted to it partly under Coleridge's authority; as in Coleridge's "Dejection" ode:

> To thee do all things live from pole to pole
> Their life the eddying of thy living soul

of which I. A. Richards wrote that *"eddying* is one of Coleridge's greatest imaginative triumphs: an eddy is in something, and is a conspicuous example of a balance of forces." True; but in Blackmur's use of the word the balance is no good unless it is desperate.

So far as I know, Blackmur never commented in print upon his own poems; but it would be odd if a critic who concerned himself with contemporary poetry had not his own in mind occasionally when writing officially about someone else's. I have often thought that Blackmur's review of

Allen Tate's *Winter Sea* was a reflection upon a predicament common to both men: besides, they were friends, and we know they held much the same understanding of poetry, an attempt "to achieve the possession of experience in objective form." I now quote a passage from the review and ask the reader to try replacing Tate's name with Blackmur's and testing the consequence upon these poems:

> [Tate] knows two things, which are complementary, that order is imposed on chaos and that chaos is the substance of order; the order is real and the chaos is actual; poetry is the means to knowledge of the complementary relation between the two; and Tate would be the first to admit that the poetry often outruns the knowledge just as he would be the first to insist that his poetry is troubled by knowledge that has not quite got into it—or has gotten into the rhythm without having transpired into the words. That is why, perhaps, so many of Tate's poems have in them a commotion that agitates in obscurity without ever quite articulating through the surface.

I have only a minor quarrel with those sentences. I do not understand what Blackmur means by saying that in some poems the knowledge has got into the rhythm without having transpired into the words. My sense of Tate's poems, and of Blackmur's, is that their rhythm is the supreme test; if the rhythm is right we can be sure that the knowledge is everywhere, suffusing the words. If the rhythm is sullen or reluctant, it means that objective form has not been achieved, knowledge and experience have made nothing more together than friction. It is my impression that in Tate's poetry and in Blackmur's the commotion beneath the words is about equal, and that the amount of inchoate or untransformed knowledge is also about equal. Sometimes the knowledge in Blackmur's poems is not his own but what he recalls of Hopkins' knowledge:

> Where was your feel for a shoaling keel,
> The shiver and shawling, yawing of doom?

and of Eliot's knowledge:

> Where then are we?—we lookers-on of art,
> outsiders by tormented, wilful choice,
> condemned to image death in each live heart,
> and kiss it so—and how shall we rejoice?

But mostly the knowledge is his own.

The poems in which the commotion reaches the surface and gives the possession of experience in objective form seem to me the following: "The Cough," "Wind and Weather," "A Labyrinth of Being, i, v, vii, ix, xi, and xiii," "Three Poems from a Text," "Scarabs for the Living," "Phoenix at Loss," "Miching Mallecho," "Sea Island Miscellany, ii, v, and vi," "October Frost," "Ripeness is All," "Phasellus Ille," and "The Rape of Europa." On the whole, the achieved poems are short. Blackmur did not go in for the large-scale organization of his experience: he worked in the poems by samples, epitomes, concentrating the energy at one point. Some of his best poems sound as if they gave the gist of a novel, not merely the plot but enough of the specific aura of the action to epitomize the relevant feeling in the case. That the poems are not novels but five or six lines of verse is the result of imaginative concentration; the gist is all the poet wants:

> There is, besides the warmth, in this new love—
> besides the radiance, the spring—the chill
> that in the old had seemed the slow, the still
> amounting up of that indifferent will
> in which we die. I keep last winter's glove.

For all we know, this poem could have begun in a poet's play upon rhymes for "love": "glove" is not improbable, even as the last word of the fable, if you allow for a complication, a detour (chill, still, will) in which the love takes on a sinister history and ends in need and self-protection and irony corresponding to the expansiveness ("There is, besides the warmth, . . .") of the beginning. In any case there is a revelation in the words, and it makes no difference to us whether the poem stirred in Blackmur's mind as an idea, a desire, a fear, or (my own preference, for once) a rhyme.

To bring these remarks to an end, I quote "Phasellus Ille," one of Blackmur's ripest poems; an imitation of Catullus' poem rather than a translation. The main effort of our attention will be to find Blackmur precisely through his response to Catullus. First I give the Latin and then an English crib; thereafter, Blackmur:

> Phasellus ille quem videtis, hospites,
> ait fuisse navium celerrimus,
> neque ullius natantis impetum trabis
> nequisse praeter ire, sive palmulis
> opus foret volare sive linteo.
> et hoc negat minacis Hadriatici
> negare litus insulasve Cycladas
> Rhodumque nobilem horridamque Thraciam
> Proponitida, trucemve Ponticum sinum,
> ubi iste post phasellus antea fuit
> comata silva: nam Cytorio in iugo
> loquente saepe sibilum edidit coma.
> Amastri Pontica et Cytore buxifer,
> tibi haec fuisse et esse cognitissima
> ait phasellus; ultima ex origine
> tuo stetisse dicit in cacumine,
> tuo imbuisse palmulas in aequore,
> et inde tot per impotentia freta
> erum tulisse, laeva sive dextera
> vocaret aura, sive utrumque Iuppiter

>   simul secundus incidisset in pedem;
>   neque ulla vota litoralibus deis
>   sibi esse facta, cum veniret a mari
>   novissimo hunc as usque limpidum lacum.
>   sed haec prius fuere: nunc recondita
>   senet quiete seque dedicat tibi,
>   gemelle Castor et gemelle Castoris.

Now a rough-and-ready translation:

> The pinnace you see here, my friends, claims that she was once the fastest ship, and that there was never any timber afloat, under oar or sail, which she could not pass. And this, she says, is vouched for by the rough Adriatic coast, the islands of the Cyclades, the wild Thracian Propontis, and the dark gulf of Pontus, where the boat started as part of a forest; for on the slope of Cytorus her leaves often rustled. Pontic Amastris and Cytorus rich in boxwood, my ship says that you know all this; that you saw her standing on your summit; that you saw her oars flash in your waters; and that you saw her thereafter carrying her owner over violent seas, first to lee, then to larboard, sometimes Jove filling the blown sails. Finally, she claims that she never called upon the protection of the sea-gods all the time she was sailing from the farthest sea to this clear lake.
>
> But these things are past. Now she rests, retired, in old age, and dedicates herself to you, Castor and Pollux.

Blackmur's poem (see p. 43) is an allusion rather than an imitation, and even further removed than an imitation or a translation from Catullus' original. Although the essential feeling is transferred from the boat to its owner, Blackmur makes no attempt to render the nostalgia of Catullus' "sed haec prius fuere: nunc recondita." Nor is there any equivalent to the irony of reported speech (*ait, negat, ait, dicit*) playing against the direct speech of the narrator. Blackmur's poem is really a postscript to Catullus'; now the feeling is entirely secular, as if the poet were to go even further than the "neque ulla vota litoralibus deis" of Catullus: presumably Catullus' meaning is that the ship retired voluntarily and perhaps prematurely from the dangers of the sea, making the traditional *vota* unnecessary. In Blackmur's poem the experience of Catullus' ship is internalized; it is already in the speaker's voice, he knows the sea without going to it. The poem is composed of such knowledge:

> if the tide lift and weigh me in his scale
> I know, and feel in me the knowledge freeze,
> how smooth the utter sea is, underneath.

These are the Blackmurian lines. It is typical of his poetry to separate knowledge from its object, or to fear precisely that separation. What the poem enacts is the fear of frozen knowledge, knowledge that has lost its bearing and its nerve before it has taken possession of its experience. In a later poem Blackmur writes

> I will not look under beds
> with stiffened eyes, knowing what I shall see.

It is another version of premature knowledge, frozen in its certainty because determined to find it in a formula. I mentioned, some pages back, Stevens' remark that Blackmur fails as an expositor of ideas "not for lack of ideas, but for not knowing what his ideas are." But I propose to deflect a little the force of that remark by saying that, whether or not Blackmur knew what his ideas were, he took every precaution to prevent that knowledge (such as it was) from becoming too sure of itself. It was not that he despised ideas; though indeed he was more concerned with feeling at a stage somewhat earlier than that in which it settles into the ripe old age (nunc recondita / senet quiete) of ideas. Santayana wrote of Emerson that "he differed from the plodding many, not in knowing things better, but in having more ways of knowing them." Blackmur thought the difference crucial. His poems, like his essays, are efforts not to enlarge the scope of his knowledge but to practice different ways of knowing things. Poetry and criticism alike were for the sake of knowledge, to keep it alive by exercising it in many different forms of life.

FROM JORDAN'S DELIGHT

From Jordan's Delight

i
Redwing

What is that island, say you, stark and black—
A Cythera in northern exile? sung
Only by sailors on the darkward tack
Or till the channel buoy give safety tongue?
   Here is no Eldorado on the wane:
   New Sirens draw us in, in silent seine.

Men do not come to live here, but to spend
Memory, time, and the long sense of flight,
And find by spendthrift each one image friend
That might outlast him and himself benight:
   In spending tides, spent winds, and unspent seas
   Find out the flowering desert dark, soul's ease.

Redwing was driven so and so drawn in,
A bearded fisher in his own annoy
Hearing without all hallowèd within,
The hermit prison-crying in the boy,
   The broken promise cutting the inward grain,
   The heart throstling the sweet-tormented brain.

Redwing was jilted forty years ago;
What wilted waits for water still, what winced
Still tenders when his fingers free and fro
The mooring-buoy, and he, each fair tide since,
   Full-bearded, full awry, takes second sight
   Of exile in the black isle, Jordan's Delight.

(Once I was with him, he within me yet,
When while the ash of dawn was colding through
And the ashen tiller stick was creaking wet
He sang of Oh, the foggy, foggy dew!—
    Then felt, and lost, the long, low-running swell
      That buoyed his words up, voice that made them spell.)

All broken ground and ledges to the east
Awash and breaking, this island has a loom
Never to be forgotten from the west
And never to be left without sea-room.
    O Redwing, by your ruddled beard I swear
      Jordan shall wreck you yet, and wrecking spare.

This stony garden crossed by souring cries—
Gull bleat, hawk shriek, mouse and eagle screams—
Retrieves, O Redwing, silence in your eyes:
It is excruciation that redeems;
    Redeems, O Redwing, by your blood I swear,
      The still brain from anhungered sirens there.

ii
The Foggy Foggy Dew

O Jordan young Jordan O sailoring friend,
I'm sailing for ye that sailor no more;
Though the moon's shut in and sun shut out
And all the sea's a drifting shore,
Though tide-rips clout and put me about
And the lather of cross-slops crab my oar,
I'll sail her true and 'cordin' to;
—And oh, the foggy foggy dew!

Where were your eyes that day, young Jordan,
For the rocking rise, the glimming land-loom?
Where your ears, my gooding boy,
For the smalling seas that shift the shingle?
Where was your feel for a shoaling keel,
The shiver and shawling, yawing of doom?
Your grandfather knew, and so now you;
—And oh, the foggy foggy dew!

Your first grandfather first, young Jordan,
Old he that in his shipwrecked thirst
Sucked sea-fog off his aching lips
And sucked but caking salt—and slaking
Followed voices on the sea.
As then came you, now I askew;
—And oh, the foggy foggy dew!

Hear now, young Jordan, salt that you are,
Where was your dread and where now mine?
The trough and the surge, the urge of the dead,
These are our manna, salt for wine.
O heaven-swell, O passing-bell,
Hearing I know ye, all ye spell;
Hold me true in long haloo:
—And oh, the foggy foggy dew!

iii
All Things are a Flowing

Flowers do better here than peas and beans,
Here nothing men may save can save its mark;
Reason a glitter flowing blues to greens
Beyond the offshore shoals gains ocean dark.
   The poor within us climb the cliff and stare
    Through second eyes and are sea-beggared there.

Sun warms the flesh, but in the marrow, wind;
The seagulls over head and neater tern
Scream woodthrush in the birches out of mind.
How warm a marrow cold enough to burn!
   There is no shelter here, no self-warm lair,
   When every lung eddies the ocean air.

All's weather here and sure, visible change;
It is the permutation of the stone,
The inner crumbling of the mountain range,
Breathes in our ears sea râle and moan.
   And this the steadied heart, our own, must bear:
   Suncalm and stormcalm, both in breathless air.

Here men wear natural colours, mostly blue,
Colour of fusion, shade of unison,
Colour of nothingness seen twice, come true,
Colour the gods must be that come undone:
   Colour of succour and mirage, O snare
   And reservoir, death ravens in arrear.

iv

Con coloriti Flori et Herba

O flowering mosses
Flowering stone
Above the barnacles and sea urchins
Above the lichen and washing weed
The slow heave the pull the give and lift
O fugitive
Quiet almost it is so far and freed
Translucent waters are
When the wave crosses

Above them all on the vain edge
Crawl, crawl out O flowering cliff
And look you down
Heave and give to the easy all uneasing swells
Look where if you fall
To the washing ledge
O blessed Francis

Such is the red stonecrop
The purpling pink sea-pea
The blue legume with bluest bloom
And blue harebell
Laced in the fissured dripping rock
Where if you fall
Falling and calling

Tenacity of fingers
Of suddenly resourceless eyes
So frail so far O Francis
This and the flowers are
So long it lingers
This good and evil chance is
You batter and you blessed drown

v

Midlight the Stable Place

Below the southern, seaward ledges, where,
Such is the heavy weathering away,
No flower grows, no silence hearts the air,
Each rock gives slowly from its utmost bay,
    There comes the day's calthumpian, all afleer,
    In his midwaste quotidian King Lear.

His great moonface rumridden and windshot,
His voice the cleaving of the wind to sea,
He drives full speed head on and sets his pots
In his own image and without a lee,
   Safe in the backwash of the ledge at bay,
   An act of God who does not die this day.

It is midwaste of breaking and the foam,
Midblack the upward curve, the flecking lace,
There always order gives disorder room,
There always midlight is the stable place.
   There in the blossoming of waywardness,
   O stalwart Lear, you eddy and confess.

vi

O Sleeping Lear

Wayward the wind weighs
For us who merely be
Westly on warm days
Eastly to rough the sea

Here wayward fishers come
Full twelve on the rock beach
To split a salvaged drum
Red rum and ruddy speech

Here one came all undone
Shirt out and jaw askew
Slipping jarred his gun
And blood ran ruddy too

What blood was that what gale
What yelling, belling cry
What signal in wind's wail
What fading frosting eye

Wayward the wind weighs
For us who merely be
All steady north these days
And no mirage asea

The blessed man got up
From rum and lobster ran
Huge to the north cliff top
And giant there began

Heaving the island down
And heaving the boulder word
Earth clods wood red, root brown
Until he fell and snored

Who shall the sleeper mock
Who smoothe his thinning hair
O eddy of whorled rock
O eddying headlost air

vii

Cythera without Disguise

It is the place of exile we divine
Will be uncovered in this ocean dark,
The place in all ill falling that we mark
Bottom: the drifting place in rock and wine.
   Look there, the closing of the sea in night,
   The falling of all human dark, eye-bright.

Ah, Dorothy, deny me if you can;
Here on this isle, exile and ever home,
This Jordan spating the full sea to foam,
Deny all that is inmost and no man.
   There's no revulsion, but certain undisguise:
   The fear, the Siren, birth in extinguished eyes.

"Ah, Dorothy, on your isle I find upright and just
Only the gibbet where there hangs our double image.
Ah, Lord our common God, give me the strength and
                                                           courage
To contemplate this heart this flesh without disgust."
    Here to my ghost of need provide expense,
    All ravening seed, all summoning violence.

x

All Sirens' Seine

Here under Jordan's seamost ledge
On splintered shale and chowdered sand
Always it is gulf's dragging edge
Where we await highwater stand.

Here all the tides of Sirens climb,
Borne upwards from the settling waves,
Borne upwards and over and back,
From spring to neap, and each its slack.

How sing they of our washing graves,
How lift and draw us in, how heave
And buoying snare us in heaven's seine,
Who in our dying parts still climb,
And falling strand our living gain.

The rising and falling, lag and retrieve,
Sun heave and withdrawing,
Moon lift and imploring,
The spring of hours and neap of time,
The drift, the range, spindrift, the soaring:
What bench-mark harks the ever change?

All waves are angel messengers
Horizon outwards and away,
All steady swells the summoners:
The voices in us where we sway.

They are the crying spites the ear,
The silence in us, all the fear,
Ringing where we cannot reach:
The nothing-hope that cravens speech.

Savour of first tear
Clamour of last denial
Wolf-need and hunger of trust
The aching all-folly of trial
Judgment of foam prison of dust

Cover the hush; all we have lost
And have believed, annihilate;
Cover the nothing that is there.
Here on this rock and rocking beach,
Uncover us, we are the cost,
All that is washed inviolate
When our full tidings seaward reach.
A new nothingness is left bare.

See there upon full sea the still
Blossoming of Jordan's heath,
And on the change, all living ill:
O eddying, bodiless faith.

xi

The Journeyman Rejoices

Some irony out of the common mind,
Some wisdom gathered, and returned, like night,
Saw half-united, half at odds, the blind
Conjunction in the name, Jordan's Delight.
    What Jordan's that?—Some journeyman of despair
    Lived here and died fishing foul weather fair.

And what delight?—Some bleak and gallant face,
Lonely in words, but under words at home,
Might look, might almost see, a first wind-trace,
What hardness rock and flower overcome.
   It is the sea face that we hidden wear
   So still, rises, rejoices, and is bare.

Of Lucifer

i
The Seed

Renounce, O Lord my God, renounce for me,
O giver-up of life and love and ghost,
not pride nor contumely—renounce most
the bitter-sweet sin of gross humility;
that taken, and annulled, from memory,
I might, reprieved from wanhope's whipping post
and half-consuming fires, once more be lost
in imperfection and necessity.

I need no Lucifer, O Crucified!
to bush the light that blossoms in my eyes,
no Adversary to out-pride my pride;
there is the animal welling in my thighs
that, over-weened, out-towered by his own need,
spends his intolerable, unappeasable seed.

ii
The Trope

The weather, and the earth that suffers it,
the water, and what the waters bear and hide,
these, and the burning stars, together lit,
O Lucifer, the meteor of my pride
in my own sight; that is, the soughing trees,
the rise of a calm tide, the covered ledge,
the star-height thought in minutes and degrees
made me Apollo new to the light's edge.

My island knowledge mounts—such is my fright—
a continent, and mounting raises me
upon a windless, sealess, starless night
apart. Grant, Lucifer, my fall may be
like thine a meteor burnt in its own light;
—and all take cover in a fallen sea.

iii
The Fruit

Ah, Lucifer, the mind is lonely, love
still lonelier, that knows the soul is thine;
all given things must be as treasure trove
received; all taken, dug from the soul's mine.
It is the looking-glass makes evil-browed
and cold the isolated self reviewed;
it is discovery that makes pride proud,
the crying out that echoes solitude.

Therefore we turn to thee to feature forth
for us, as in an actor's strut and voice,
the needs that all unadded add our worth,
that, bottoming despair, let us rejoice.
    Thine, arch rebel, these words, thine all we lose:
    the sum of vain hopes that we cannot use.

iv
The Entropy

I have lain down, enacting emptiness
within a sleep: heaven is empty so,
a sleep without the body's sloth for dress,
without the wakened loss the mind must know;
have risen up, resuming the bright blood,
the pumping heart, still brain, and feasting eye
and am thus sheathed and trapped in solitude:
a separated life that still can die.

How shall I ponder these in the cold stream,
the wordless and unsummoned sense that springs
indifferent beneath all words? Which dream,
humble or proud, shall smoothe these sufferings?
   Ah, Lucifer, this is the truest hell,
   where death alone shall be impossible.

An Elegy for Five

When I lay sick and like to die
five chosen friends came out to call;
for each I put my bottles by
and arched my back against the wall.
The live man visiting the sick
within him finds his own death quick.

Each was embarrassed, and the first,
who could not give his hand the most;
he kept ten fingers tightly pursed
to clasp his own half-given ghost.
His whitened knuckles more than mine
showed how death climbs live veins, a vine.

My friend believe me, even you
for whom all friendship is caress,
no hand can ever touch the blue
background of others' nothingness.
As night horizons close the sea
in you death closes death in me.

The second brought a singing voice
as if, such was her rising fear,
she might by heaping noise on noise
delude a little her inward ear.
Hot with the longing in her brain
her pink shells reddened in refrain.

And now my friend believe me, death
that ends voice, has none of its own;
no slightest sibilance of breath
can ever give to silence tone,—
nor friendship ever in a word
escape separate silence heard.

The third kept taking from the air
half-savoured morsels of disease,
the hope that garnishes despair;
and tasting swallowed all his ease.
Upon his purpling lips I saw
death rise ruminant from his maw.

Believe now, friend, this is the gist
of old friendship and all its savour:
the unpredictable last tryst
when neither feeds on other's favour,
but each can in his salt blood taste
the sea that rising lays us waste.

The fourth put lilies in a vase
to mix the scent of their distress
with mine, and prayed the two bouquets
might fuse themselves, and coalesce.
Immovable, her nostrils meant
she smelt herself, intent.

Believe, now more than ever, friend,
odours are omens on the air,
signals that interchange and blend
solitudes they cannot impair.
Death, as it signals us, perfumes
the ecstasy the flesh resumes.

The fifth, by grace, came late at night
when I was thoughtful, and his eyes
absorbing mine absorbed their light
and the dark image that in them lies.
Across his naked face he wore
the long shudder of one death more.

Wherefore, my bitter friend, believe
friendship that wears to nakedness,
like life, like hope, leaves least to grieve
and most, O sweet unknown, to bless:
the sight that proves each man alone—
unknowable death, as such, made known.

For Horace Hall

i

This man was yours, O Death, these fifteen years:
he who had been best dead when gassed, in battle,
was mortgaged out a kind of living chattel,
for a late funeral and rehearsed tears.
At one side of his grave there stood his wife
and the three girls he spawned of dead man's stuff;
three Legion buglers blew, for his cast slough,
a mid-day taps. There was no drum or fife.

Now, Sire, you have him, may your majesty
lecher again beneath his striped shroud;
let us who must remember him, now see
upon whose service we stand here, bowed.
    That much we earned when his expiring breath
    removed from us a fifteen-year-big death.

ii

Wilson, the man was yours that April noon
you saw your people's clutching hand as mailed
and, to the bluster of a British tune,
the passionate peace of Jefferson was staled.
If Page and Colonel House were gulled by Grey,
you, poor Messiah, were worse gulled by them:
content you on this loud inglorious day,
this dust the soil you spilt on Clio's hem.

The man was yours, is dead as you are dead;
like you, who in the textbooks of the schools
gain glory daily, of him it shall be said,
likewise: Always, in death, the hero rules.
    God grant we know, and never know again,
    your lives found ignominy sovereign.

iii

The sword comes first to mind but not to hand;
the argument was bloodier and the game
much slower than the sword can understand
unless the blade be twisted out of name.
And so it is the man is yours, O Lord,
twisted by rule until his blood-drenched lung
made mustard gas seem more the threatened sword
than Saladin's when the true Church was young.

But yours as well, O Lord, another way;
this scapegoat of a scapegoat might heap up
his after-knowledge on a pyre and pray:
his the last blood in the armed idol's cup;
    the last, in nineteen hundred years' increase,
    Prodigal of that Lord who brought, not peace.

iv

Let public feeling go, there Horace Hall
lies in his fortune and his country's flag.
Lift him, it is the weight of death will fall
and in the bottom of your belly sag.
Touch him and in your bowels the new cold
is not imagined but a manifest—
that you, oblivious, already fold
and nurture a cold passion for cold rest.

What hope is that you swallow, seeing death
put under earth and firmed with prim, saved sod?
What hope that saps you like a fear? What breath
is that which leaves you, leaving a full fraud?
    I think that each man dying sows the wind
    and we the dry seed pods he leaves behind.

Sea Island Miscellany

i

The tough sea island sheep
towards dawn break up our sleep;
may they attend likewise
the death we do this day put off—
with the faint, fog-cracked cough
of half surprise.

ii

Brown in their summer cowls
above the tidemarks live
the weasel mouse and owl
from the second of breath
to the second of death
and never raise an eye
lest they grow fugitive
(so watching likewise I)
and, salt sea-mortified,
there be no room to hide
no earth in which to die.

iii

One hundred feet of cliff,
two eagles over that;
climbing, that nightmare, If,
got on my back and sat—
that hand and foot might know
two eagles were, not nearer
but like the sea below
iminently sheerer.
I, clutching the cliff,
embraced the nightmare, If.

iv

Nothing moves much but the tide
in this mid island thoroughfare;
stillness of rock on either side,
a gull here and a white heron there.

And the gull skims when the tide falls
over the herring down to sea,
and the han breaks heavy wings and calls,
slow-vanishing, thrice raucously.

What moved in me left with the birds,
and left one thing to think upon:
so I, in three unspeakable words,
cry thrice my own oblivion.

v

One grey and foaming day
I looked from my lee shore
landwards and across the bay:
my eyes grew small and sore.

Low in the low sea-waves
the coastline sank from sight;
the viewless, full sea-graves
stood open like the night:

(sea waters are most bare
when darkness spreads her trawl,
the sea-night winds her snare
either for ship or soul).

Once along this coast
my fathers made their sail
and were with all hands lost,
outweathered in a gale.

Note: Second stanza, third line: "han" or "great han" is the Maine coast familiar form for heron. *Hamlet* has "handsaw"; other forms are "hernshaw" and "hern."

Now from long looking I
have come on second sight,
there where the lost shores lie
the sea is breeding night.

vi

Here are we in the blown sea-spray,
quick salt in the breath we breathe,
sea-violence strikes the day,
and her soft falling underneath.

But do not think I hold you so
because I love you or because
the billows with their come and go
toss us together like two straws.

No. I am afraid lest you
be bare as I am, lest the sea take
from you as me, and then you, too,
stare naked where the first seas break.

vii
Half-tide Ledge

Sunday the sea made morning worship, sang
Venite, Kyrie, and a long Amen,
over a flowing cassock did put on
glittering blindness, surplice of the sun.
Towards high noon her eldest, high-run tide
rebelled at formal song and in the Sanctus
made heavy heavy mockery of God,
and I, almost before I knew it, saw
the altar ledges of the Lord awash.
These are the obsequies I think on most.

viii

Some days the lobstermen
make me their company;
riding the sea is then
arduous intimacy.

Observe old Danny Watts
reach with a rumbling laugh
after a ducking pot
and hook it with a gaff,

untie and empty, bait,
and with one body-turn
cast the netted crate
over the side, astern.

—The morning's business
too quickly overcome,
my lubber's earning is
to have been made at home.

ix

Mirage

The wind was in another country, and
the day had gathered to its heart of noon
the sum of silence, heat, and stricken time.
Not a ripple spread. The sea mirrored
perfectly all the nothing in the sky.
We had to walk about to keep our eyes
from seeing nothing, and our hearts from stopping
at nothing. Then most suddenly we saw
horizon on horizon lifting up
out of the sea's edge a shining mountain
sun-yellow and sea-green; against it surf
flung spray and spume into the miles of sky.
Somebody said mirage, and it was gone,
but there I have been living ever since.

x
Sea-Odalisque

East of the eastern ledge a hundred yards
the haddock feed on rising tides, and there
I choose a round warm room, walled in fog,
and let my dory anchor go. I hear
only Nash Island's friendly signal bell
and sometimes, distant, from Petit Manan,
a lonely horn dying out, lost, and dull,
creeping along the waters under the fog.
Though I have fish enough for chowder, still
the oars lie straight and quiet along the thwarts,
and likewise I. There is no hurry on this sea.
Languorous kelp and seaweed drift me by,
three porpoises whirl up their flukes astern,
a seal emerges from the grey ground swell,
regards me slowly, slowly submarines.
The boat makes slowly north and south, slowly
rises from trough to crest, as slowly settles.
This is the lulling of a lullaby.

The tide of hours comes to its full, and I
wonder why men abuse their flesh with mermaids,
image sea-nymphs and such like fictive things.
There is the sea herself, her long low swell,
in my own room, spreading her lazy thighs.

xi

All day my dog runs up and down
the fury of the surf-line, meeting
the crumpled havoc of each breaker
with the cowed fury of his own greeting.

There is in his retreating bark
what I feel only after dark.

When we get home he will, I think,
deaf with the sea's indifferent roar,
vociferate the morning mailman
with harsher fury than before.

xii

With evening the fog grew brown
behind me on the browner land;
grew grayer where the sea was gray,
grew and moved, like a closing hand.

Three shag flew seaward by
to gain low-water slack
above some deep-sea shoal;
pursuing eyes went black.

Had it been clear I had been still,
the shag beat past and nothing stirred,
but in the hollow of this grey hand
all moved, like an unspoken word;

moved without motion, moved
like a reaching hand, down
upon the fallen tide:
moved till I thought to drown.

A fishboat made the head and turned.
The fog seemed less, somehow withdrawn
before the brawl of gulls astern;
waving, I felt the great hand gone.

xiii

Seas Incarnadine

Wind was not, flat was, but was imminent.
The long grey swells reddened with the dawn,
I saw the black spar-buoy on Leighton's shoal
lifted on red water and dip from sight.
The breaking of the seas below was dull.

I on my cliff stood up in all my blood
confessing the sudden murder in my heart
to the dark tangle of rock and spray beneath.
Had I friend there I would have cast him down.

Red vanished and the shrunken sun sky-lost.
Like mountain night wind was, sheer-fallen, black.
I could not see nor hear nor breathe, but held,
sea-crucified, back-nailed against granite,
wind-fast, tight-drenched, flat-flailed, a sacrifice
vainly surrendered to unpropitiable seas.

Seas would not take me. All I saw of glory,
where twenty fathoms broke gigantic black
backs to shrieking smother, fathoms in air,
made me run out of blood entirely. I was
the only prisoner in a world set free.

xiv

Where shall I go then
if all I wish is going,
what must I know then
if all I need is knowing?

Sea answer is sea-deep.
Look at the sea and sleep,
ever waves are furling
over and under and back
furling unfurling still furling
over and deeper and black;
look at the sea look down
under the tidal sweep
dark waters are
a still black star
and drown

xv

What is treasure for
if I am always more
than any treasure, less
than any nothingness?

Sea answer is sea-sand.
Look at the tide's bare hand
then at the flotsam trove
it scatters in this cove,
a melting jellyfish
a sailor's wooden dish
and an old galley stove
content on the bare sand.

xvi

Pray for a night-storm
pray for an open sea.
Hidden upon the land
the body will be warm,
while the soul, cold and free,
raises a bare hand
over a full sea.

Judas Priest

i

Come let us gather up the hated men,
the true outsiders: those with the tireless eyes
that watch new bloodshed waste god's death again;
those with the fault of memory likewise:
all those who shun the dogma's dreadful weight
and know the ignominy of applause,
who see the plastic strategy of state
resolved into the tactics of a Cause.

These are the printed faces none can read
who feel god loves them most: these stand aside,
free creatures of necessity that seed
the slow words out: Behold what gods have died.
   Though the blown blossom petals in thin air
   the seed survives, the grown thing in despair.

ii

We who have had no part in hurried act,
no share in the willed hydra, hope, shed blood
no less, no less wear out our fortitude
with sweat and rage to keep the natural pact;
we too have seen the unemployed attacked,
the forced, foul ill of scabs, seen hunger lewd
in bright eyes on the pot of terror glued:
seen, in the mirror, each his own soul sacked.

Let them be desperate that hope, let them
be absolute and sweeten violence;
let them by rote and frantic apothegm
swear we outsiders earn but Judas' pence.
   —Yet Judas made a mirror of his will
   where both the horror and the hope stood still.

iii

Judas, not Pilate, had a wakened mind
and knew what agony must come about;
while Pilate washed his hands of all mankind,
he saw necessity past Pilate's doubt.
So driven mad did he alone indict
the waste the terror the intolerable loss,
the near abyss of darkness in the light,
and made a live tree of a wooden cross.

Where then are we?—we lookers-on of art,
outsiders by tormented, wilful choice,
condemned to image death in each live heart,
and kiss it so—and how shall we rejoice?
   But if men prophesy Gethsemane
   regardless, there must some regard the tree.

iv

O comrades of a simpler faith, think now,
it is compassion in us that prevails:
beyond the dogma is the sweating brow
and in the living wood the driven nails.
This Judas knew and forced himself outside;
wherefore the ignominious act occurred
not by mob's cry but by the final pride,
the terrible compassion of the word.

What is it shivers in the sun, beheld
above an early breadline in late spring,
O comrades! but the human dark that felled,
for Judas, safety in imagining.
   Who but a Judas, a willed looker-on,
   can cherish light until the dark be gone.

Views of Boston Common
and Near By

i

Sometimes, as if forewarned, before we die
colon bacilli half-eat us on the sly
and rot the rest. On Chardon Street this night,
between outrageous heart and sober eye,
the breadline slowly inchworms out of sight.

ii

These are my enemies, the men who doze
the noontime out along the asphalt path,
pale pupae in the sun. My midnight grows,
as I lie small and naked in my bath,
like theirs, new prey to every wind that blows.

iii

O beggar beggar try your art on me.
False insolence will strike on falser pride.
Be sure though that as palm leaves palm you see
that you no more than I can ever hide
our unsuccourable inward beggary.

iv

At every subway port a Sally stands
collecting for the poor a brief thanksgiving.
Observe her feet in newspapers, her hands
in woolen gloves. Such charity demands
even of dead hopes that they go on living.

v
The Burial Ground

Only the dead are faithful, for their trust,
despite the iron fence, the iron doors,
and living grass, like them makes vacant dust.
Lie still, lie quiet, O my ancestors:
you cannot rise, and we the living must.

Witness of Light

See all we see
weakness and strength
without feud without faith
mirror the mystery
light in the light

See all we see
horror in hope
torment in power
form without scope
faults for a tragedy
lightning in light

See all we see
boredom of lust
desiring desire
the terror of justice
resorting to fire

See all we see
the breath in its flight
the oppression of peace
the hunger for bloodshed
and rape as release
false home in the night

Humbled from confusion
the cumulus words:
O charitable heart
see all we see
the witnessing art
light in the light

October Frost

The comfortable noise long reading makes
brimming within the inward ear,
at midnight stopped like a sharp cough,
like a warm garment taken off.
I heard the kitchen slowly creak,
unsettling all its ancient gear,
and saw beyond the lamplight loom
the further darkness of the room.
Life was a draining out, until,
need and custom joining will,
I went outside into the night
where in the moon the frost was bright.

Cold in the temples, cold
lifting the rooted hair,
it is the new cold
quickening the richened air.

Across the mudflats of Flat Bay
the tide was moonwards making way,
and on the water's rising edge
among the eelgrass and salt sedge
the endless rustle and soft clucks
of a thousand feeding ducks
made a warm noise about my ears.

Quiet, I crept between the tiers
of young white birch. But a stick cracked
under my foot and a duck quacked
loudly in the comfortable night.
Like wind breaking, their thousand-flight
soared up. Transfixed on the bright ground
I filled with the full frost of sound.

Steriles Ritournelles

I saw a face rise up
made honest by the dark
shadow of its hat;
what animal out of the ark
but would continue chaste
had its opposite a face like that?

—How have I seen this promise waste—
treasure of company,
complement in thought,
the cord of unity
binding the public deed—
spent, bewildered, broken—gone to seed.

How have I seen a smile unsought
startle the mystery,
make plain how all this action ends.
From this his gestured generosity
I think him such an actor as, may be,
might lay down a hated wife for friends.

Petit Manan Point

At last from the thick mile of brush we six
came out to sea-light in our summer tan,
came out on the last flat hand
of seaward land,
issued in eager company
on the full solitude of Petit Manan.

This land is falling
into the sea
is sliding is sinking
receding is bleeding
year by year
is drinking the deep
killing salt
of the sea

within the natural seawall's granite rise
this that is marsh and soft bog to our feet,
with blue-flag waving and creeping cranberries,
once grew three hundred acres of black birch,
their backs to windward, and bent hackmatack.
Regard the red wood-earth torn bare, and there:—
sea-strangled, gibbeted against the sky,
the last grey splintered trunks and crippled thumbs.
Ghostly, these gestures are beyond repair.
—And here, upwards upon the sea, a snarl
of huge ship timbers and stove-in lobster pots,
great stuff and small, a thicket of sea-slain
a thousand stumbled yards in length, ten wide.
Here one could lay impossible keel and frame
for half the hulls upon the Gulf of Maine.

Muscles a month made limber
in sun and earthly use
went dull and loose;
like the shivered ship timber
southeast to south southwest
muscle and bone made wreckage in my breast.

Without counsel or despair
or any hope of haven
(behold like a long last breath
in this flat hand
the laying on of death)
each made a separate
hard path his own
among the snarled rubble of wood and stone
to a small eminence, and sat;
and was himself, alone, driven
into the place of bones.

Ask other lands redress
for injured imagination,
deracinated flesh;
pray other lands for peace
on wounded memories.

Beware this bleak elation.

This is the flattened land
this is the touched horizon.
Stand up. Assent. Await
the mountainous white waste
of the great storm to come

Three Songs at Equinox

i

I in my stillness cried aloud,
keep that man blind,
leave him his slavery,
who from brooding on his kind
memory out of mind
presides a sightless effigy
upon the night-dark streaming crowd;
have mercy on that mole
whose darkness is his soul.

ii

What of the active hand, I cried,
driven by dreamless will
to add unconscious pride
with each access of skill;
that gains great learning
whether by sun's caress
or remote burning
under cool flesh.

Grant that it last not out its use
nor hang a broken tool
upon a winter nail,
but come suddenly to its end
without memory as false friend
or hope's abuse.

iii

He whom this stillness breeds
rejoices with a roving eye
on thistles blown to seed,
on hills against the sky,
until in the sun's late haze
the wild, neap-tidal air goes cold:
hill and thistle equally old.

May those eyes, still bright,
come at the last,
day being past,
to see their own night.

The Cough

He

Suppose I coughed; would I
because my ribs and stomach give
with each explosion, live
more surely in your inward eye?
Do small infirmities
raise knowledge, or stir sympathies?

She

Cough while I think.—It is like this:
a pattern at the panes
assures me that it rains.
The difference is,
between that patterning and you,
unless you stop you'll have me coughing too.

He

Yet when I speak you hear
in the flat sound the singing sense,
and are full audience
of all I turn in my mind's ear.
Consider, a cough should sing
as clear, if equalled in imagining.

She

You have a sad philosophy.
Will nothing teach you true:—
of all that passes through
our intimacy,
only the shared thing endures.
Speaking, you speak my words as well as yours.

He

We speak God's words, no doubt,
and in communion drink God's wine,
never yours, nor mine.
But the god lessens and dies out,
the chancel rail turns trough
with use, and the bread stales. I'd rather cough.

She

Cough if you will, your purview's blind.
The magic of old phrases
in rehearsal but amazes
more the full mind:
and the deep hush within them comes,
hushing the voice, like the hush after drums.

He

Address your homilies
elsewhere. You'll have me thinking, Madam,
myself a fig for Adam,
and you, with your pomposities,
a wooly-nightgowned Eve:
when I'll do all my coughing in my sleeve.

She

Forgive yourself your rhetoric:
none else can understand
the sleight of his own hand,
or be self-sick.
—Words verge on flesh, and so we may,
someday, be to ourselves the things we say.

He

Mayhap. But God forbid
there seem more beauty in a word
in that it's said, and heard,
than lies in the still body hid.
Seeing full flesh advance,
and live, to your mere word I'd cough askance.

Phasellus Ille

This little boat you see, my friends, has not,
as once Catullus' pinnance could repeat,
a history of deep-sea peril sought;
for her no honoured peace, no earned retreat.
Too narrow for her length in beam, unstable
and unseaworthy, her strakes and transom leak;
although no landsman, even, would call her able,
I float her daily in our tidal creek.

I do not need the bluster and the wail
in this small boat, of perilous high seas
nor the blown salt smarting in my teeth;
if the tide lift and weigh me in his scale
I know, and feel in me the knowledge freeze,
how smooth the utter sea is, underneath.

Scarabs for the Living

i
Quem Dixere Chaos

Each finding fleshly piety accursed,
no wonder Christian ages, in despair,
saw God with neither flesh nor winey hair.
O Aphrodite, Dionysus, spare
from my sight, him who came before ye, first.

ii

Soldier, consider well these animals,
the lion, lamb, and rat, and how each falls:
indifferent goat of human sacrifice.
Dear Sir, on thee this weasel glory lies:
to be with music ratted in blind walls.

iii

Beat on, O colding heart, beat firm, beat true,
until at last your own night throbless come
and the slow warmth you lost, that warmed me through,
shall warm your memory over, coffined home.
Meanwhile I coffin cold I have of you.

iv

O Eros, who so long gave unabashed
the outward-flowing, uncorrupted joy
and were less seminal god than generous boy,
why worm you inwards now, self-gnawed, self-lashed—
must I be one of them the gods destroy!

v

O sailor sailor tell me why
though in the seawine of your eye
I see nothing dead and nothing die
I know from the stillness seething there
my heart's hope is my soul's despair.

vi

To meditate upon the tiger, turn
your human eyes from his past-human stare;
beyond his cage a pigeon tops an urn,
beyond the pigeon falls the twilight air,
and there, steadfast, he sees a viewless lair.

vii

Lay down one hand before you like a tool
and let the other, in your mind, grow strange;
then let the strangers meet. Who but a fool
or a passionate man, thinks loss is blood-exchange,
if the cold hand should warm and the hot cool!

viii

Think now, O rediscovered, old-faced friend,
what bourne it is of which we cannot tell,
our silence being its only dividend.
Think now, it is the same upspringing well
plumbed in the beginning-word, drunk in the end.

ix

Hermes the helper praise, who had approved
the rainbow prayer and sent, as godly slaking,
lips that were heaven-wet, earth-warm. Awaking,
soft from the long fall, praise him for taking,
his own, the dream whence help had been removed.

x

May you who have been watched, observe
that as watched stars fade and the sea
thins to a line illimitably
it is the same bottomless reserve
I fasten on in you, you me.

xi

Within this windless covert silence drops
leaf by leaf and birches make bare bones;
a startled woodcock's whistling flight new-stops
the wind beyond the woods, and I, alone,
feel my still flight trembling into stone.

xii

There is, besides the warmth, in this new love—
besides the radiance, the spring—the chill
that in the old had seemed the slow, the still
amounting up of that indifferent will
in which we die. I keep last winter's glove.

xiii

Become a woman whom I could not know
she turned, a blight upon her own renown
(I too a stranger suddenly ingrown)
and gave, wooden and like a mallet blow,
one shout that brought obscene horizons down.

xiv

Pride is the thing outside,
pride is the itching hide;
the proud man out of doors
goes naked in his sores.
Forgive him that he shrinks inside.

xv

Smugness is the first reward
befalls impatient certainty—
your world and you are in accord
of mutual unreality
at rest; the last is being bored.

xvi

Oh, I was honest in the womb
where I had neither time nor room
nor any secret hope to hide.
Now there are love and work this side
of honesty, two hopes that lied.

xvii

Oh, love is lusty blind
but wakened is abased;
in darkness kind finds kind;
in daylight, double-faced,
each frees the inner waste
umbrageous dark confined.

xviii

Once in the monarch darkness, you, by blood
at mountain height exalted, and wine-wooed,
wine of the closing eye, made body's need
spill on the blinded moment the soul's seed.
Which was it, soul or body, was withstood?

xix

Humiliation is an apple-tree
with worms; humility the wasting sea.
Eat of the fruit as dished. You know the look,
you wear it, of Adam whom the truth forsook.
The proof of Eden is Gethsemane.

xx

The chickadee-dee-dee is not a bird
like stilted heron fishing minnie pools
that in their fleeing shriek the sky like fools;
the chickadee (dee-dee) is most a word
to keep the thicket warm when summer cools.

xxi

It is the coward in me will not rest,
but eddying against the coming time
exhausts the prayer for safety dime by dime.
It is the coward sees the double crime:
where blood unleashed is nonetheless oppressed.

xxii

The subaltern resentments, waste and need,
made hanging bother at my door, a crape
for fusty hope of which the dead are freed;
and now I also, love: you are the gap
within me, paradise and no escape.

xxiii

It is the slow encroachment, word by word,
of sleep upon the wakened mind, the slow
manoeuvre of unseemly vertigo,
whereby disease in order is inferred;
and in the sleep a blotting fall of snow.

xxiv

Quiet the self, and silence brims like spring:
the soaking in of light, the gathering
of shadow up, after each passing cloud,
the green life eating into death aloud,
the hum of seasons; all on beating wing.

Since There's No Help . . .

What of the beauty that these hands have held,
is there no help that they preserve it still,
and can be seized, as when great silence welled,
more than a memory, almost at will?
Is there no help, if I see in these eyes
the drunken weather of the headlong heart,
the radiance of wordless intimacies,
brim to the flood? It is no help to part.

You, Michael, were but righting wrong with wrong.
Why should I pocket my imploring hands,
why seal my inner ear to inmost song
or quench the radiance in which she stands?
   Such would be parting: an insensate night
   that perjures, with its pain, the soul's delight.

Simulacrum Deae

Having admired, and in admiring sired
desire, the firm long line from waist to knee,
having by accident and warmth of wine
suddenly let my eyes go free in hers,
I stopped, seizing within me the stilled second
before the threatened thunderclap occurs.

Slowly I turned, thunder about my ears,
the suffering of wonder in my eyes;
she who had been half handsome stranger, half
casual friend, that second had become
a face for desperate homage, and amends.

I looked and she was newly flesh, her arms
intensive, calm, and round, her eyes likewise
fresh with the first ease of intimacy
burned through their own darkness to the light;
and I began to think with lips and eyelids,
with all the tender motions of the body,
sharp or confused, in loin or fingertips,
that may, guided, encouraged, firm the mind
to meet the crisis of another's being;
and with the greater, aching tenderness
shaking in unspoken words, unseen seeing,
wherein there is no purpose or disguise,
only a blind mind discovering a blind.

—How sweet the torment in this structure joins
the hope that monuments its own despair.
The trembling animal inside my loins
inside my heart my head my soul rose up
to search the inscrutable fastness of her being,
to seize only the face that was not there.

Pone Metum . . .

Be not afraid, Cerinthus, the gods harm
not those who wear each other's love for charm—
or so Tibullus wrote in secret dread—
but those who venerate a passion dead.

Be not afraid. Did Goethe fear
when with the sun the day's love set
to see the moon's new love appear?

Be not afraid.
The agony to be possessed
to hide and give hiding
to be naked undismayed
to find at last abiding
the mind's comfort and the blood's rest
without let:
all this shall seem bravura yet
and the slow charm be lost.

O my Cerinthus, then be not afraid
though all your being crumple and come unmade.
Be not afraid, if in the great fright,
for all the ravage and the sack
and the black frost,
you find on a moonless night
yourself intact.

River-Walk

O friend of shadow, friend of brimming silence,
come walk with me, come slowly by my side.
We shall, if we walk long enough, and turn
as the sun turns us, burning in our eyes,
at last see the red river fold that sun
to rest, and have ourselves such peace of earth
as evens out those strangers, night and day.

—Did I say peace? Exhaustion is not peace,
only an incapacity, a fraud
whereby the flesh betrays itself to sleep
waking to unrelenting replenishment.
Death, or its equivalent in knowledge,
that is the peace our blood and bowels bid for;
that is the peace drenches the checked heart,
checked by a face, a word, by wind or rain,
by the self coming fully upon itself.

Yet walk with me, be by my side, and speak.
It is a compact then? You will be free?—
and talkative?—and easy in your flesh?—
all these are needful to the speaking sense.
And you will walk so gently on the turf
the earth will move a little upwards, gently
fall a little with every last footfall.

There's more than that though here. There are the birds,
maybe a shining hundred redwinged blackbirds
singing among the birches till we come.
They did not know and could not sing our song,
nor is their silence our despair. We are
(in this desert judged, impeached, identified)
the straight shadows of separated stars.

O friend of shadow, friend of silence, speak.
(Look you do see us firming in the sun:
a bright looming in air that hesitates
withdraws returns verges upon the flesh
and is the shadow in the whitest light.)
Speak now: of the harsh April grass spirting
out of the burned land, of the winter dust
already loosening along the road.
I do beseech you put behind us all
that dark silence from which we came. Speak now:
Conjure out of the ragged black of crows,
sentinelled and awkward upon the alders,
at least the gloss of ravens; let your voice
fall soft among those sunken willows, bringing
their generation's promise of slow dying,
at least for us, to tardy bloom. Speak now,
or we shall hear the bottom of our silence
echoing.

Dedications

i

Ripeness is All

I knew that lust would pall,
blood would not always run
a ripe and bursting ball
down to the aching groin.

I had no need to will
passion on passion spent
if common life could fill
vigorous hearts content.

I who have treasured less
the fury and the foam
than devout tenderness
studied out at home,

this night have slowly heard
unhappy ripeness reach
from heart to groin to word
drenching each with each.

ii

Wind and Weather

The heart exaggerates. I have not lost
despite the wind and weather, no, nor shall,
more than the heart must lose, no more at most
than when a thief cries thief, no more at all.
What can be shared seems never a full share
until by justifiable grand theft
each in his guilt has tenderness to spare.
Only of what I stole am I bereft.

That which was once, is now again my own.
It was my own affection stolen back
that seemed so sweet, the known returned unknown;
I gave that I might measure my own lack,
she hers. The rest was social wind and weather:
the storm that forced still holds our lives together.

iii
The Spear

There is no recourse for the mind
in rhymed, disjointed prose
nor luck in self-sent valentines
although the arrow and the heart
be redder than the Virgin's rose.

Salvation is a salmon speared,
the ancient Fisher cried,
sprung from the spring torrent
without right or warrant
safe from the great safety of the sea.

Leave me my Odyssey,
the living soul's hyperbole,
peril in which to hide,
peace for my naked eyes.
O let my heart
that spurns satieties
be living hooked from the fresh flood
but let my soul rehearse
without benefit or curse
of a saviour's blood
its difficult and dangerous art.

I shall be dead and rot
a full four-seasoned year
until my last beginning is rubbed out
in the deep-bit Christmas frost
before my ghost leaps ripe
for the Fisher's spear.

iv

Of Mind's Silvering

There is a mirror the mind's silvering
perfects moment to moment in slow eyes.
Looked in they show no tarnish of surprise,
resentment, or despair; their mirroring
takes and returns, without rendering
the murky homage of shared injuries:
there is, before each image shifts or dies,
knowledge without contact unbewildering.

Or so we plead—we who have married reason
on desperate cause, when the heart's cause was lost,
to live without wealth and without cost
free of blood vengeance and blood treason
until, reason a proud deserter too,
the light the night at last break both ways through.

v

The Witnessing Eye

Serenity comes not
from reason or the mind's control,
only an anguish of things forgot
investing a blank soul,
only an eunuch's love
frantic in the holy grove,
only a widowed thought.

Ending unending
giant immersion
flood-lost dispersion
the seizure the release
the torment the blending
the enemy, the peace

O saviour the shadow
the having of blood of life of light
to give out, assent to, and lose,
the saving engraving memory.
This be serenity
to the witnessing eye:
the abyss, the rejoicing by night.

A Labyrinth of Being

i

I saw a boy, once, put a thinking hand
across eternity (the pasture bars)
slowly and touch, almost, the horse's nose;
and the horse baulk, then nuzzle patiently.
So I would enter a friend's house. So I,
each in its time, would enter love, would die.

ii

Because one face had meant
exile for a year
to manual labours of the heart,
exile from the mind's content
the mind's slow-moving certain gear,
he lost the patience of life's art
and settled in that corner
where the soul is disciplined and taught
by memory the mourner
how much more bitter than dead beauty is
the funeral business
of the holy ghost of thought.

iii

My dear, flesh is the eagerness
of the full heart to speak, forgive
if it may seem to leave
as much to curse as bless.
What dumb man with a new-found tongue
but speaks out wildly and too long?

iv

Breakfast we hardly share, but spar for peace;
we still are heavy in the night's adventure,—
the long travel of sleep, the soul's release
from sign and countersign, from time's indenture;
hence in our orisons ask, not God's grace
but immediate courage to meet a wakened face.

v

Three silences made him a single word:
the footloose lover's agony of eye,
the heartfast husband's peace; these joined the third,
the straight silence of something about to die
that something else, no different, might live.
They sat in silence on their separate chairs
knowing that silence would be positive
when they should climb their nightly Goodnight stairs.

He spoke it first. Is it ourselves that go
from us? ourselves that to ourselves add up,
because this child shall be, to zero?—No.
(Her voice was from a void that broke.) We stop:
we are not us: not dear and dear: we are
to this child's sun the silent morning star.

vi

We prayed our sleep
might reawake us
deep night to deeper;
behold our sleep unmake us.

Dark even in darkness
rose that secret sleeper,
loom of our fathers' dust,
he who is now our keeper.

We lay in peace exhausted,
calmed with each other's need;
we spent for heart's delight
and spent our living seed.

We warmed the darkness through,
we sought eternal hiding;
now if this child be born
it is our own death, tiding.

vii

This marriage has insatiable, sad eyes
which looking once, enough, are yet unsatisfied,
needs must still peer until long peering prize
mere peering priceless—vainglorying pride.
What devil's here? It is the marriage knot
our eyes, fast-craven, crave us to untie
then see what's tied, what's not.—Though gordian-cut,
still devil-tied, it snubs satiety.

Look further and there is no knot, because
there never was one till we said it so
reciting a daft dozen of old saws.
That devil's absolute for action though:
I look again, immediate this, not far—
I am, she is, quick glance, caught breath: we are.

viii

Because the elm-tree buds are red
in sunlight, yellow brown in shade,
I think not of a living thing—
my dog my wife and most myself—
but that I think of it as dead.

Because the harrowed land is black
and the wet wales ashine like flesh
in sunlight, dull blue steel in shade,
this much I do expect and hate,
I shall be fertile so when dead—
fertile and indiscriminate.

ix

If out of disappointment I let go,
losing the skill of silence, a low cry,
it's not that courtesy is gone, not so:
the formal life goes on though substance die.
You may, since learning blood exacts blood-cost,
set up a bloodless tit for tat, commanding
the tin parade at will—content that most
intimacy stops short with understanding.

In me the substance lies not dead but hidden;
nourished from beat to beat in the heart's night,
lies still and hushed till it again be bidden
forth to the shocked silence of the light.
    Thence, where untimely thou art thee'd and thou'd,
    beyond word-knowledge, broke that cry aloud.

x

This is a bold thing we see,
mixing our shadows in the sun;
I look at you, you look at me,
and swear our shadows may be one.

This is a grave thing we do,
nerve to nerve we faintly bleed;
you look at me, I look at you.
Our souls go early so to seed.

This is a dark thing we do,
face the darkness side by side;
you look at me, I look at you.
Now there's nowhere else to hide.

xi

My friend, what brothers us in each?—I take,
most mine out of the wordling worlds we bled,
not life, but what is takeable, the dead.
I say the dead. Things cannot sleep nor wake
nor grow nor lessen, upleap nor ever slack,
which have been changed between two selves. I said
the dead—what's not but *was*. This struggle-bread,
the pressed wafer of knowledge, this I break.

I eat the past, the matter we have been,
and so eat god, a fast; devour my part
in you: Yet you're untouched. You say that's so
of me?—my dead selves only you draw in
your often eye and seldom smile? Live heart,
we walk the earth ahead of all we know.

xii

Indubitable Venus

After each debauchery
flesh that I serve and foster
sinks crippled on one knee
and prays a godly wraith
to resurrect and bolster
the blind urge of faith.

A snowman is more nothingness than snow,
passion once shaped should be imagined dead.
Let then my body, grovelling, believe,
the soft-earned discipline of self-deceit
is the one mastery it may achieve.
I that would judge, more than my body, know
(as a cold hope is desperate to entreat)
a cold lust is a dreadful thing to bed.

I who can doubt
and doubting earn my keep,
who can rejoicing weather out
the irony of intellectual storm
and stilled desire,
doubt not my dreaming loins require
(indubitable Venus on each night's tide of sleep)
bravado of feeling warm.

xiii

By Luckless Blood

Soft to the river falls the millet field
moulding and giving to the wind, as might
an ordinary woman slowly yield
by moonlight her own summer to the night.
Alas, this tardy love that comes elate,
irradiant sun-flash on cresting seas,
invades and wastes, as if by chosen spate
not luckless blood, my quiet granaries.

I am at loss, all manners and no man,
all aching breath, all queasy near the heart,
the fond brain vacillating plan to plan:
all's torment here, dull hope, and under-smart—
   unless, O sweetest harvest, sleeping flood,
   the old love grow in me and find me good.

A Funeral for a Few Sticks
Three Fragments from an Early Poem. 1925

i

I sit here, and this man sitting beside me,
Both thinking, thinking a form upon the world.
Here in this hillside place this ancient man,
Whom I in my own might have dreamed alive,
This man and I, and we alone, guarding
A fire, and he feeding the flames with sticks.
His weathered, earnest face, his earnest voice:
Stuff of my thought. Of these I made a god.
—But did my heart beat truly when I dreamed him?

It is no matter. I have walked with him
All day, and heard him speak, and penetrate
That secret sense which lurks beneath the skin.
I saw him stare, when he had finished talking,
Gravely across the bare brown hills, and felt
The everlasting quiet of the land
Drawn up into my veins, a numbing sap.
Then he and I were breathless images
Rooted eternally into that stillness.

I heard him speak, reduce his flesh to voice:
"If on a word I hang the sum of time,
If on a name I nail the sign of years—
All wisdom passes on my breath, and dies."
The voice snaps in the memory, a vain
Recoil. "Sweetness is only to the worm."
I made this man an oracle, to hear
The stroke of being, beat on the heart's gong;
Gave him the colour of a god, may be,
That he might make the godly seem more real,

That he might sheathe the shadow of our dream
With human flesh and human memory.
Being matured among the dead, he sprang
Among the living old, and glitters where
Old thought becomes a sense, the sense a voice.

ii

I have pulled up this man from darkness, singing
In the long aisles within my mind, singing
Upon the everlasting years, singing
Till my whole being grows giddy on the song.
(A song of timber cut and timber burned,
Of sticks which beat the earth before they burned.)
I have imagined him above the game
Of memory, beyond the treachery
Of fancy, real: a thought grown mountainous,
Gigantic, become a gesture and a man.
I made him so his eyes might meet the sun,
And in that blazing mirror lose his image,
Then stare us through with blue, sunbrightened eyes,—
Yet never cringe among our deadly shadows,
But rather greet each shadow separately
And call its name, and burn a stick for it.
I'd therefore have him choose out of his pack
One stick for me, and while he burned it up
Have him sing out those words which had been mine
From my own mouth had I had song to sing them.

iii

Again dark pours; flesh on the bestial floor.
—And if I chuckle sitting on this ledge?
(The seeds of laughter burst in stony fruit.)
I sit here and my god beside me drinking.
"Drinking drinking drinking
Sups sips quaffs twelve bottles a case."

What have I said?—Bring up your god on whiskey
And feed the flames on whiskey. Say that's justice,
And say that ends it. Chuckle once again.
And the flesh reels and shakes with voice. You lose
Order, and time is vanquished; lose all faith,
Die out, depart this world. Still in the head
Within the glutted brain, a film or mirror
Holding the world most steadfast. Say that's justice.
—I sit here, sit here. Shall I muse?—collect
Records of infamy?—maybe display
The ruck of gravestones I have left behind me
Upon the thin curtain of memory
In lifeless view?—myself my audience
Hearing in my unprofitable laughter
My spoken epitaph?—A dullard's ending.
I sit here.—But in the court of bones what mercy,
The judgments of a dusty wit. "O you
Who sit there prisoner at the bar, you
Who squirm in the stuffy scarf of memory,
Beware all human gifts. By this discharged . . .
The Court in consideration of your offence
Awards the palm to youth;—that twenty years
Spread out through ninety husky æons."
(You could have floored me with a beery breath.)
O dusty Judge O Wisdom of this Court
The worms are slavering within your robes,
And by this sentence O mine enemy
I gain a name, The Worm Among The Courts.
. . . But some one grinned. An aggravated case,
Her aggravating legs. (The Worm swelled up
To go to Court.) Besides, the grass was deep:
"The Court in . . . thirty days, one hundred dollars . . ."
And is my father in this bar room? Look
Under your feet. O father kiss my feet
And close those marble eyes and wipe that face
Battered from a thousand buck-and-wings.

John Doe and Richard Roe, the bench of bones:
O Dicky Dicky darling hold your tongue.
The musty mockery of broken bottles.
—Get off those swinging doors.

I said I'd chuckle. So much for epigraph.
I sit here with my god, a case between us;
A garrulous antique choirboy of a god.
See no pale nymphs to-day; nor homely wives
Spreading acceptable bodies in the dark;
No dogface demon women snare my legs:—
I snatch the pure mirror of shadow, enter
Among invisible reflections, emerge
And see my selfsame face stare back at me.
—How shall I profit here, when this my god
Wipes out even the dream?
How shall I prosper when my god brings up
A bulging drunken monster of ourselves
And sets him murderously before my face?
"May be he comes, this man, an answerer
To all your hope. See where he lurches past
Shaking the foul red staff before him. Hear
From the raw lips the words that bubble up
And spatter on the air so that the air
Crackles and smarts on the tautened eardrums.
What issue thence in sign or warming?—This:
In him words lose all lien upon the mind
And cloy the flesh like lice.—This image swells:
Some wench puffed up with a hundred measures of
Such slime as his staff spurts, took you to bed
And stewed you in her sweat until you rotted
Inwardly. So he mumbles from a mouth
Stuffed with such memory. Look you, his face
A metamorphosis of yours and mine,
Another mirror to our stricken souls."

Towards morning once I heard him speak most slowly,
Whose body seemed the last thing on the earth.
"Put flesh, all human flesh, away, for flesh
But binds the fever on the bone and sheathes
The naked thought in a live winding-sheet.
Put blood, all human blood, away, for blood
Is but the sweat that your heart's agony
Drains from the bitter virtue of the bone.
And with the flesh put sorrow, with the blood,
Desire, away. Treasure the sweetened bone.
Nothing but wind speaks in your gaping vents.
—Do this, for you are old, and memory
Bloats you, obesity on ancient bone,
Sorrow the bland accomplice of desire.
Do this, for you are old. But hope that some
Miraculous bright day your bones ascend
A glittering shaft of dust into the sun."
—So in his voice my body thinned away.

THE SECOND WORLD

The Second World

Who that has sailed by star
on the light night-air,
first hand on the tiller,
second, the nibbling sheet,

who, looking aloft and then aback,
has not one moment lost
in the wind's still eye
his second world
and the bright star
before the long shudder fills on
                    the windward tack?

Missa Vocis

Priest-mannerly the mind,
that president mask,
gives dogsight to the new blind,
priest-mannerly unknowing
what mastering ear-task
keeps the great churn going.

O unmannerable heart,
monk-dancer, be still,
be leashless, apart:
the sounding, the growing
unabettable will
sets the great churn going.

Lie chidden, lie dark,
in the reserved deep
lie prone, lie stark:
the unprayable flowing,
the vast sluiceage of sleep,
sets the great churn going.

In the wringing of new sound,
chance flowering to choice,
old words in full round
in-breathing, thrall-throwing:
the mass of new voice
keeps the great churn going.

Una Vita Nuova

That crazy wretch got up
and donned sea-going clothes.
"Tomtit," says he, "tom tup,
how lately blooms the rose!"
So instinct runs away.

That tireless fag went out,
the sea was spattered sun.
"Such goodness all about
and I am overrun."
So instinct skims away.

That hireling in arrear
sat down to ease his legs.
"I wear man's tiring-gear,"
cries he, "and nothing begs."
So instinct pours away.

That tired miser fished,
his livelong self as bait.
"I've caught before I wished
the flounder in heaven's strait."
So instinct scales away.

He turned, all flounder-faint,
in hope of human eyes.
"All beggar, all complaint,
all pierced I am," he cries:
all instinct skun away.

For Comfort and for Size

"Ten years aborning I,"
the young man in me cries,
—"my house is empty best."
The old goat in me spat,
"Go beard the graying rat."
Between us thus we try
for comfort and for size.
—But who prepares the guest?

"Ten years too soon I'll die,
and all those years are spies
—they wrestle in my rest."
"Instead of prayer cry Scat,
and lecher in cold fat,"
said the old boar in the sty;
"odd comfort and even size!"
—But who prepares the guest?

"Ten years too late I'll dye
sea-blue these changing eyes
—truth is the thing expressed."
"Dye dark, self-dark, and drat
the glass you're looking at."
Homeless, the sea-lights wisp by,
willing the gloom we prize.
—But who prepares the guest?

"Aye wing-and-wing I'll fly,
night airs abaft me rise
—and all ten years confessed."
"Your sails," said he, "will slat,
your gear tear tit for tat."
All greeting, no reply
he meant life was. He lies.
—But who prepares the guest?

Rats, Lice, and History
An Image of the United States Senate

There is no precedence between a louse and a flea.
—Dr. Johnson

That man who keeps the diary
is there, his eyes like running mice;
Ambassador plenipotentiary,
he says, to bargain fleas for lice.

Who sent him? whom he bargains for?
or what he'd sound like if he spoke?
or look like if he closed that door?
all's doubtless written in his book.

But we don't know. We only know
he's here, his hand upon the knob
of the big door. The rest we grow
aware of, like an engine throb.

He's not a senator, that's sure;
none of the page boys even see him;
there's nothing about him to endure:
you don't want to delouse or flea him.

—Is it the odor of almonds creeps
down the aisles, between the rows,
heavier than air? than sleep?
that each man smells but never knows?

Or is it the belling sound of words,
The vision of mankind that you see,
that can be only overheard,
is my vision's greatest enemy?

That's why the senators can't keep still
but each one, conscious of his face,
unconscious of his driving will,
scurries and squeaks from desk to dais,

and he who has been recognised
(anyone can be, somebody must)
looks on all fours, and undersized,
gnawing darkness like a crust.

That man who keeps the diary,
suppose he opened up that door,
would he be live, be you, be me?
be recognised upon the floor?

Or would the bitter almond rise,
the rising gorge of full ill ease,
and all the lice, as each one dies,
take precedence with all the fleas?

Most like that door's a solid wall
that cannot open save it fall.
Most like that diarist's the ghost
that speaks the actual we have lost.

Before Sentence Is Passed

i

I have this to say, if I can say it.
Things are undone, your Honour. We are the same.
You also, Gentlemen: bench, box, and bar—
the same with different vantages. This is mine.
—Here are my hands upon the rail, my voice
fretting your ears. The wood is sticky, my words
the tight quality of the air you breathe,
the air a cauling skin upon us. All this
that is dismay in you, in me disorder,
develops, envelops, this browning twilight air,
this room of screams and patience and rejoicing,
and hides without day the uncreated face.

(But look, Gentlemen, so good, so true:
These two fat bailiffs will catch me if I fall;
the Court keeps order, and you yourselves
observe decorum past your understanding.
Consider, the will you keep, in me
is voluntary, habit a conscious act.)

You will agree, and well within your time,
that nothing I can say here is digression,
and if you do not think so now, Wait:
You have not felt the focus closing, firming
on your vantage, not quite heard safety stop.
You don't know whether, right now, your watch
    has stopped.
The time will not be wasted if you look,
even if you look also at the big clock over
    your heads.
—My digressions are like that: inward occupations.

To be in a new place and tell the old story,
to fumble in the voice and say, "It is not so,
this rubbish of insurrection, treason, thought,
I stand here charged with," that would perjure me;
—oh, not in this Court nor in your Honour's law!
My innocence, like my guilt, is radical,
and strikes a taproot down you cannot sever.
There is a face within me that coheres.
It is not easy to portray that face,
to prefigure what is long past, to show
the normal as a monster, to arrest God
visibly in his invisible escape;
to exhibit love as uncreated fear.

But what is hidden without looking may yet
transpire without being noticed: You shall see
as you saw, just now, your watches were not right.

ii

Asserted righteousness is avowed guilt,
Gentlemen: the mercy within your bowels
attests it, and the cold in the whites of your eyes.
Verdict-cold. This is an interdicted time.
Conviction—yours as well as mine—and yours,
your Honour, too, becomes the formal cry
we order up to cover the blank moment
saying, It is the Law. And if you ask—
and may it please your Honour, *you* should ask,
(for goodness and truth look not askance but boredom),—
Who interdicted what? I answer so:

It is my people, all my race and time,
the stuff I harbour, salvage that I am,
that gradually have lost in tension, lost,
that is, the keeping sod on the hill farms,
(for we are hills at heart, whence cometh help),
and with the loss found various perfidy

of white hope and party-coloured withdrawals.
We have the forced, exhausting, unreplenishing crop.
No more. Ripeness is lost: which is tension itself.

Even the apple has lost its tartness, and
the potato cooks flat with no taste of death:
good chiefly for alcohol, intoxication.
But I do not wish to exaggerate the thunderclap
who did not feel the lightning strike. It is simple:
Erosion of good and evil, that's the phrase;
no tension to hold them together, no tragic need,
only the raging and indifferent perfidies
of opinionated unconvicted men.
Thus we clutch for untenable positions.

Your Honour knows just what I mean, and you,
my Gentlemen, are no more puzzled than I.
I am as dizzy with plain facts as you are:
the federate battle of the frantic dead.
I too am distracted from this lower buzz.
Bats raid in the vault, I know, and gnats fly.
It is the evening; and in the actual world
which has neither faith nor perfidy nor hope,
it is the hour when eyes and ears take count
of vestiges and intimations, and
the gyrations in which these are merged and grow.
It is the sound through the open windows, high up.

—I need not remind you that we do not live
much in the actual world;
                          and hence, Gentlemen,
the sensation of irreducible distress, never death.
Take care, take care, you do not fly out the window.
The bats do, gnats do not—they settle,
sludge next morning in the residue of oil
(if you remember one generation back),
their distress always unequal in distribution.

It makes little difference that what is irrelevant
to gnats may be the next actuality for us:
the mass in darkness, the falling, the wiping up:
the deceit of fire seen only as light
or the worse fraud of light put up as fire.
You choose the phrase; I am the prisoner who sees.

But let us avoid that perspective. (I see a fly
rummaging the discolored crease of that policeman's collar!)
This has become a very quiet place.
One feels a dislocation. One tries at last
to say only what the heart says, do only
what the buds do: flower by conviction:
the inward mastery of the outward act.
Is it a gulf, Gentlemen, this place
of falling off? Look, it is cloaca,
in either case the end-all and inter-regnum
where every issue joins and none cry out.

But all this is confusing, flies buzzing.
(Confusion: have you seen confusion when safety stops—
the miring of draft horses in the salt marsh
below the turnips?) One lets go only
what one has not held, the roughage of the mind.
One holds
only that which was already reserved,
the vestige brought out of turbulence, order
surviving only by digesting disorder:
the gravel in each mouthful that we eat.

Such fustian! unless imagination supervene
with items, like your faces looking at mine,
your minds employing the words I employ,
your situation seen as the under half of mine:
my situation the guilty reward of yours.

iii

It is like houses burning, here in this room,
right now, or soon, with all these people, my people,
swaying as I sway, and each thinking slowly
of his own house, not far off, afire by instinct.
The flues are dirty or the wiring faulty.
We think of little things,—of drafts and fuses,
of faces in the cut-off windows,—as large:
the unfinished work, the unattended wife—
as large as that! That is our history:
a holocaust of inattention, just
put out. It is in this sense that I burn.
It is your inattention set the fire
—oh not your present glare, your aching look
beyond, behind, the look to get away
of minds made up, and lost, while unawares—
I mean your inattention to yourselves,
until you saw me looking at you with both
your eyes and mine.
I doubt not you saw red—the beginning
sin of safety, the lower rim of blindness:
not only not to look, which may be forgiven,
but to act without looking, which is perfidy:
the final ignominy of giving in.

So you have come here, Gentlemen. So I.
And so your Honour. And all these people came,
a crowd sprung out of the cobbles, because of us:
the ever-springing hope of new guilt.
By this time, I think there is not one of you
feels quite at home. The first strangeness gone,
the new not wholly come. Even my bailiffs
grow tired with waiting: their eyes begin to creep.
There is disorder, like heavy breathing in the next room,

like people making way when no one comes.
The rest is not silence, except for me.
You will see shortly, all of you will see:
It is my right: I stand here in your stead.

The Cellar Goes Down with a Step

If I ask for your confidence, citizens, think:
You can't give what you cannot retract; not this year;
nor go forward unless you are ready to sink.
You prefer, therefore, this: that we speak but small beer.

The indubitably minor intoxications are
my religion and yours, whether I swear or affirm
or just plainly depose in full voice at the bar:
The people in the cellar have cause for alarm.

If you ask What people? What cellar?—I blench
(in my own cellarage) and uphold—Education:
the new need that I see for schoolboys to learn French,
the frank language that ends mere conversation.

It's the natural thing, not at all disconcerting
nor suspicious, my friends. Our American flag
is not plainer than the mediate wave of mere blurting
if we speak only English and carry eggs in a bag.

Many thanks. You have heartened me, strengthened
    my cause,
you young men with straight eyes, older men with
    improved looks;
your indifference marks the last reach of applause.
I can speak this once safely and speak by the Book:

In the cellars of cities, of factories, hotels
and courthouses, condemned houses, and planned towns,
on the first downward step, we begin to know well:
the other fellow never does the walking up and down.

The Idea of Christian Society

> It is not the effort nor the failure tires.
> The waste remains, the waste remains and kills.
> —William Empson

The acute old men may refuse to read Dante,
yet like him they connive at the dead while alive,
this peekaboo inside us; let it be
for they also have sharp faces, play stud penny ante
looking twice at each face card and holing each ace
this hugger mugger rising; let it be.

The unquiet, the not knowing, the lessening sun,
anæsthetic accord; Dante's face like a board;
this peekaboo outside us; let it be
the small boy in his bed; winter owl where rats run—
Look! the bright mezzo-mark, the white swoops
    on the dark!
the hugger mugger's in us; let it be.

But the old men keeping store have no time for ill reading;
the boy's dying; the owl rising; new rats aprowl;
this is the hurly burly; let it be

and the time has neither gone nor quite come for good
    breeding:
we admit being bored and void the quick word
this is the hocus pocus; let it be.

Does the cold owl, the small boy, the grey rat in the run,
O false Dantes, need most the uncomfortable ghost?
—unless the peekaboo inside us; let it be.

The Dead Ride Fast

Nobody ever galloped on this road
without probable cause. Nobody wants
false wind in the face at a dead end.
Nobody wants, this day, his hair to grow.
No one would disagree about that, unless
to cover up deeper agreement, hide
the robber's sense, the pounding, the vertigo,
the confusion under expert discernment:
all we leave out to make of faith a hope.

And if you think I am not talking about anything
it is because you have not looked out the window
where I wash and shave and sometimes trim my hair,
and have not seen the inviolable standstill
everything comes to, people, horses, cars,
beyond the little rise above the culvert.
It is that standstill finds all coming things
between the woods they come from and the rise
where, recognised, they seem already here.
With me it is no longer a matter of not looking
or whether this day everything comes at once;
because of that eddying standstill I am,
expectant, reverent, or suddenly degenerate,
always deliberately unprepared.

Perhaps you don't catch what I mean. Look here.
There have been bats in this house, variously
crawling and flitting, not easy to get out,
but always bats whether you knew them or not;
there have been seabirds beat against the window,
bill on, some die, but mostly only stun;
ducks in the marsh, with their known unknowable voices;
also telegrams delivered at night;
all these are wholesome until you stiffen to meet them.

You understand: I will not make of politics
a superstition, of religion a distrust,
of thought a mania. I will not look under beds
with stiffened eyes, knowing what I shall see.
I will look at horses, people, cars, look up
from shaving, and the hurried dead, look up
through the light-sodden, reverberating air—

until that day, hopeful, thoroughly prepared,
in my own glass I trim my snakey locks.

THE GOOD EUROPEAN

Twelve Scarabs for the Living: 1942

i
Terror Treed

Where courage shaped at manhood left me freed,
now clearer freedom is, and sweeter air,
in actual rejoiced-in fear, in terror treed.
It is the final excellence of despair
unfetters, and reveals, the full deed.

ii
The Skin of the Soul

If righteousness without its faith is sin
and faith without its sin is empty act,
how shall the armed man plead? or soul save skin?
Between the lover and his murder pact
there is the third lost face, self looking in.

iii
Second Drawer

Inside the desk-life of this chartered ease
I keep—that lockless unopenable second drawer—
my great grand uncle Charles's Civil War,
his cavalry pistols and his diaries.
The martyr batters at the wardrobe door.

iv
Theme for a Novel

Crossed loyalties that graze together,
new love betrayed, the old defiled,
make any an immoderate tether.
Nothing thrives here but runs wild.
My house lies open to the weather.

v
Heil!

Scream in your man's voice out
the last biling of your staff and rod.
Stand straight, click heels, up arm, and shout!
How should you know, through Christless span,
—O single-throated, singled man—
how all that foulness covets God.

vi
Declaration

The one burgling masked word
the burst sound of the self rent
is not mine nor my accord:
I come as one sent
from violate to violent.

vii
A Fresh Encounter

Again severalty falls
the vast like and dislike
the rich rage and love's small change
in the same loins
the full and fell
awake for loving use.

viii
Tush, said the Godless Man

How shall the pierced hope become a skill
or unassayable dread make a true die?
How keep an open or a candid eye
if the spider is more righteous than the fly?
My mouth makes chicken-fat of all my will.

ix
Wisp o' the Will

For eighteen years this mouth has lied:
there is no man nor woman
I can lie down beside
and cry O God give me to hide.
Never could I have cried from pride;
nor can I in humiliation will the human.

x
To Enobarbus
(the Fish-hawk atop Prospect Harbor Beacon)

Thanks once again for dark, old screamer, and
give thanks yourself, old eagle-feeder, fisher-king:
The night, full-armed, all-wiving, young, descends,
descends, O barred Osprey, upon us both
to blot the sick valiance that cannot act.

xi
Phoenix as Foundling

Ah, foundling Phoenix, from the first wing rush
will ashes fall, of all that was renewed,
the ignominy, the growing good, the hush:
recovering through change the changeless mood.
This pyre, O Phoenix, lights new-foundling blood.

xii
Enantiodromia

Note well, you who have hearted hands,
that inching, loveless lust, one detail more,
will bring you where the Vision stands:
half unexorcisable ancestor
and half your newest self, turned grudging whore.

Three Poems from a Text:
Isaiah LXI: 1-3

i
Beauty for Ashes

All day I trespassed on my friend's new death,
and talked of it with strangers to give it handle,
the skill of a firm pressure in the handshake,
felt but not regarded. "My friend was killed!"
I had the voice but not the throat for gesture,
the seething in me was beneath control.
"Was killed in Italy on a high road."
I thought of dust, and rock, and hanging trees.
"Never was God revealed upon that road,
never was man saved in that high place!"

By night private, I balanced warring moods,
white anarchs shifting in the moonlit room,
and made of fragments—his lurking underword,
straight eyes, high cheeks, and equable fresh glee—
a sheave of presences to garner home,
harvest and fecund ancestor of cold dawn.
Also, I gathered unknown waste of him
looming within, the smother lifting the wide sea.
Anarch or ancestor, mood called mood.

I have been selfed just so before, and drained.
By ill and various violence have died
at eight an aunt, an uncle nine years later;
a father and grandfather in great age;
and five friends else in swart, unequal time.
Theirs has been the chaos I abide,
of them myself the faltering piety:
my ear for echo, my hope for grace and gesture.
I am in tide with them, their verge in me.

My friend died on no road. My friend was killed
in the rude place that stirs and is the same,
the bottom place that is beyond, the place
of balance and loss, gulf in even eyes.
He died protesting fellowship and self,
the common hope, uttering himself alone.

In either ash is beauty, in all beauty ash.
Accepting all, all but the self yields up.

ii

The Oil of Joy for Mourning

Him whom the old joy fell over,
night rain each night a new lover,
I sing, I see, I wake;
in last me, the unsleeping, the dark rover—
in new him a raw joy for no sake.

2

As once by June dusk he played trover,
at full moon found fourth leaf in cut clover
among grass, dew-honey, and live toil,
so I flush new scent from hush-cover,
from the fit air we breathed, a sweet spoil.

3

Again as, through noon-dazzle, flash plover
beyond number, and are lost in fog-hover,
from his dying—the swept air and sea-slake—
I pluck, I lose, I discover
one flower, all flight, and joy-foil.

iii
*A Garment of Praise
for the Spirit of Heaviness*

How may I see the triune man at once?—
Mowing witchgrass in the quarry road
while grasshoppers clacked before the scythe
one August noon, his easy straddling stride;
or later, swimming far out and on his back,
the half-smoked cabana making long ash
beside me on black granite. Such memories
are of the country of the blue, too far
for capture and too near to see at once.

There is no choice, severalty is all
in life that has been stopped but never finished.
I see him then:
In the north shadow-pool of the opened door
greeting imperceptive friends with gravity and drinks,
and surer friends with candor only less grave—
as sunlight is grave upon a windless bay,
the warm upon the cool, like rum in milk.
He saw people more in relation than as kin;
as next, and touching, than as continuing,
like grasses prostrate in the marshy stream.
Keen on the possible, the first to hand,
but prodding the impossible, he doubted
nothing of the murder in the heart
that might—so long the distance!—be blessing in the eyes:
knowing murder in the eyes was from sacked heart.
Obliged, therefore obliging; owning disorder within,
he observed a gentleman's disregard without.
"Laurel at table, ivy would spread," he said,
"through after-talk, over the sere and sore."
He put the oldest inchoate shapes in words
that rushed, as animals rush before they spring,

to a sharp halt, cresting, then falling fell.
The quiet in his voice was drenched in strength
—always a kind of violence in gear.

A man of family, ancestors were like children:
subject to expectation, certain to disappoint,
always a part of the self—the unfinished part.
A man of state, his privilege to claim none.
An extravagant man, could not afford protection.
In talk he reached straight through what lay between
without quite reaching, so deep the pit he reached from—
so deep you could not tell what depth brimmed there.

Therefore as soldier he cast himself a rôle
that needed ancestors and children to play;
behind, ahead; dragon slaying dragon.
Folly is more acceptable if played
half by memory, half expectation,
and violence loses unreality.
"Never was an army made less career of war,"
he wrote, and wrote again as I write now,
"so safe from mockery and fond applause."
Never a hopeful man, yet he was hope,
the necessary, upwelling swaddling cry
that man's might and towering skill, man's hand,
might end what fellowed them, in single blow,
then shudder only in the birth of dream.
Man has created that one cry as good;
this shudder of it what we grieve, and praise.

Thirteen Scarabs for the Living: 1945

i
Too Much for One: Not Enough to Go Round

There are too many heart-shaped words for one
to seem enough or two to offer choice;
and yet the heart offers the mind a voice
above all words. Crying its All is None,
it is the heart itself that comes undone.

ii
With the Bit in the Teeth

Hunger makes the simplest face: the blind;
makes up the soul that outlasts fear, the heart
all beat, and a dead hundredweight for mind.
Only its mouth can see, that shapely part:
all mouthing, all slow, lock-jaw grind.

iii
Vengeance is Mine

How beautiful the kicked-in face you show
for surgery, self-heal, or burial cart,—
or manners if, by God, there be no heart.
All's maggot else, and swarming vertigo,
mortification of the victor's woe.

iv
The Socratic Method

"I cannot live," man's nearest ape cried out,
"unless my ugliness assert its good
like Socrates."—Who is in self so stout,
so plain and passionate in fortitude,
he can keep down the outrage of his own lout?

v
For an Air Fit to Breathe

After childhood there is no certain home;
boys cannot breathe the ordinary air,
and men must needs mistrust their own despair;
but as friends go, or die, or ail, there come
compassionate intimations everywhere.

vi
The Quality of Horizon Blue

Who's sick? Who lies awake in sweat?—Oh, who,
in new cut-off from speech to answer, prays
the splitting of the self will stop? Not you;
you see betimes the blackest black is blue;
where Self recedes in selves, and Day in days.

vii
In the Wind's Eye

Passionate are palms that clasp in double fist;
compassionate palms lie open to the sky;
on either the dew falls in manna-mist.
Weather is all. The sailor's answering wrist
hauls up, or down, as winds rise, or veer, or die.

viii
On Common Ground

Shambles come ready-made these years, are found
wherever man has stood, and lost, his ground.
So the wide world. It is no otherwise
within the narrow ward where each man lies
apart, his own breathing a shamble-sound.

ix
Holed Up

Terror is not in the sweet night that falls,
that covers with moon-snow all raw frontiers,
that merges shadow-hands, that shadows tears.
All that is life's self-heal. True terror crawls
within, where though bog closes, raw voice still calls.

x
Don't Tread on Me
(For Those Who Plead Humiliation)

All words are whips, but the buff-end of that word
is lead with ending echo in your throat
as well as mine; the echo we miser-hoard
like strength until the viper is full bloat.
Look how pit vipers knot them in accord.

xi
Super Hanc Petram

Such is the disrepair of love in man
this house has hingeless doors that still are locked,
has windows glazed with eyes that crave, and scan,
that vertigo in which the Rock is rocked.
When public life is all, then God is mocked.

xii
It Is Not Half So Late as You Think

Not Byron's Greece nor Garibaldi's Rome,
no Third Republic, no, not Lenin's dream,
not Ireland in the pitch; not ever these,
for these are of the dead most dead, dead pride:
all their hard triumphs our reopened sores.

xiii
The Light Left On

The light left on where no one is burns double yellow,
late light and lone: two wounds that never fail
and never heal. It burns beyond hope's pale
what hope would make, what substance would avail;
makes room, makes house, makes home, with faithful fellow.

The Good European: 1945

I
A Decent Christian Burial

A robin redbreast in a rage
puts all heaven in a cage.
   —Blake (with rhymes reversed)

i

For chocolate, for soap, for stone
at heart, men hunger and atone
in common supper. It was the war
packed wolves at every outside door.

Our Europe is their history,
their ups and downs. The man I see
makes grits of the whole Christian age,
eats of himself in splitting rage.

His hunger, which had been hope burning,
becomes the aimless, cold thing, turning.

Nausea is that beggar's crust,
love comes unswallowed in distrust;
nausea and distrust but rile
even the eyes in a black bile.

It is the eyes of that man there
we must now seal, and weight, with prayer,
since neither death nor sleep can close
lids on those final vertigos.

ii

Look: he is the man before
the after man, he is the door
either opening or shutting; he
is Eden live, and Ark asea.

Look: there is of you in him
the gone life, ache of lost limb;
he is the dreaded self you plumb:
all things that bide, and can not come.

iii
(Secreto: For All the Dead)

Yet who would want relief
from mankind's final grief?
May be my sighing
is yourself dying.
Thus we add belief
beyond complying.
May be the mired adventure
binds us to rejoice
where death is homage due,
and living on, a censure.
May be the living I
is the next risk of you,
and your dead voice
my noblest lie.

iv

Because the children mauled each other
I saw the Father beat the Mother,
the Family become the Ghost,
the faithless carry off the host.

How often has this Figure stood
exhausted in the quarry wood
breaking into stone on stone
and nothing mortared on its own:

the man intransigent: the Son
thinking himself the desert one.

Not ever yet has that man died
quite of his own will and pride,
not even at Augustine's Rome
his hitherto most desert home.

Always the officious stranger slew
(likewise his office now we do)
in holy fear of burying
the living and renewable thing.

This time he does not need us save
for extra grace on extra grave:
he is self-slain, this new begin,
this self of us and utter sin.

Stand therefore now aside, and brood
in your own desert and be renewed.

v
(*Secreto: For All the Living*)

It is not the burned out houses,
not food nor transport loss, that rouses
massive resentment and self-rape
and pleads disorder as amazed escape.

It is the ragging in the mind
as thought goes doggo, kind on kind,
and all that had been common will
is spoil divided at the kill.

Concert and conflict disengaged
leaves even natural prayer outraged.

II
Phoenix at Loss

i

There's little phoenix-clay in us, these days;
that little, more an ache than forward stress.
Doubtless the impulse always came at ebb
and turn, an under shudder at the slack,
only accountable as further loss;
so if tide rose, and not our tide, it rose
but to obliterate, above the tide-mark,
the biggest driftwood bonfire we could build
to burn all up before all fire went out.
Atlantis may have been burned, not swallowed up:
like Troy, and Alexandria, and Rome;
the Reichstag and the House of Commons, cities
within cities, whose ashes still are hot.
To say these things quite clearly and at once:
We burn the last dry lifewood of the mind.

ii

To say these things again for conscience' sake:
Suppose a cornfield by the sea afire,
one crow, one scarecrow, and one farmer there,
Mount Desert rising barren at the back.
Suppose, that is, you are at home and lost.
—Surely each Phoenix must have been old crow
in his own glass, scarecrow to the faithful,
so ancient his annunciation seemed,
so cold at dark noon his residual fire;
even his gorgeousness showed ragged black
in the fiery rage and fire-begotten wind;
seemed draggled beyond capacity to fly—
while acrid, thick, the dragon-smoke of flesh
half-suffocates that unexampled flame
in which the self utters the self consumed.

So fierce the necessary bellows are.
—Old crow, old crow, why drabble in that fire?
Can you and those crossed sticks burn as one ash
unless the mountain fall and sea make maw?
Old crow, old crow himself is scarecrow now:
the nothingness the scarecrow frightened off.

iii

Old crow, old crow, surely there's fire enough
to ash your present limit of desire.
Old crow, old crow, flop in that fire like mire
if you, or that one there, be phoenix-stuff.

Have you another measure for man's scope
in which the final virtue is rubbed out
and even Phoenix to the lout seems lout?
True sacrifice is suicide by hope.

III

Dinner for All

A good sinner makes mighty good eating.
  —heard in a dream

i

Thought is the bomb for personnel: We think,
and are a long time numb, like a thumbed bell
stinging and numbing, think and muster up
mostly incendiary reactions, think
disaster, wreaked or suffered, shapes all choice.
Explosion is contagion mind to mind,
a jelly-fire that sears the senses out,
and so compounds such felonies of faith
that plots to foul or blight
each other's peace seem author to our peace.
Thought is that bomb, and each the equal target.
(Wherefore caws the Phoenix: Let me be!)

ii

That bomb is thought, destroying thought preserved,
as if we had not always, each of us,
the crazy might to kill his dearest son
brother or friend, all but the odd man left,
yet seldom did, because the odd man smiled.
How shall we bring the senses back to faith?
how touch the various god in man? how trust
the sudden drunkenness of intimation
that keeps and teeters balance, razor-edged
—the ecstasy beyond in present love?
That bomb is thought, and each the equal target.
(Wherefore crows the Phoenix: Let me be!)

iii

Take thought more slowly, then—as tolling bells
take echoes in of our dead selves, and wound
with actuality the living ear.
Take thought of harm in love, that fends off sleep
(lest in the harm the love dream justice dead)
until their concert wells, like blood elate,
a sweetness going off, and all eyes close.
So hard thought's pattern is, and true. All things
are possible in their corruption, none
without. Love takes the risk the best is worst.
Thought is that bomb, and each the equal target.
—Wherefore pleads the Phoenix: Let me be!

IV
Coda:
Respublica Christiana

> The sea is what it always was.
> —T. S. Eliot

Here come the hole-and-corner men
straggling the night-routes once again
to loose—like rain one drenching sound—
interregnum from underground.

Eight hundred years of drifted silt
eddy above us, all our guilt.

(What weight of wind what whirling cloud
what rock what spring what birth in shroud)

These lovers in disorder must
fresh-soak the ignominious dust
that blows and blinds us in dry flood
till all fall on their knees in blood.

No order that can bind and loose
self-violence and mass-abuse,
no order that can loose and bind
the shambles under the human mind;

no order ripens into weather
unless it bind and loose together
chaos of good consuming ill,
of lovers who search and shun God's will.

I in my corner-hole wait numb,
and stinging, hope all aching thumb.
This much I say in secret now:
God does not make, does keep, man's vow.

Sunt Lacrimae Rerum
et Mentem Mortalia Tangunt

Across the huddled lamplight window glass
is black, ashine with that last, blacker mass,
the drifting shadow of arrested wings.
Here is the empty chair, and here, alas!
the awaited time, when time seems most to pass.

We are, in midmost ground, our own dead kings:

Because in dark are bred the tears of things
that frost the heart, cold dew on prostrate grass,
new psyche gathers gooseflesh in, and sings,
in its dark corners, its wild waste winnowings.

Boy and Man:
The Cracking Glass

—"Look, look in your heart, believing boy,
what is this life looming against the mind
that now, half ignominy and half joy,
even now, with men retrenching on their kind,
can pull us upwards from the underground,
your ground and mine, with such a cracking sound?"

—"Look in your vanity, O vivid man,
not in my grating heart; it is your eyes,
frosty with fallen dark and the great van
of the moon's light, which tell the noble lies
that rend us and praise rending as God's will.
Look in your pride. Create the God you kill."

—"I cannot look into that glass and pray."
—"That cracking is my life your truth the way."

Miching Mallecho

Hopping, half-flying, pouncing, by foot and inch
the crow scuttled upon the rabbit, that small
ear-flattened, brown, zig-zagging anguished winch
of sound, until it could no longer crawl.

Out of the main deep, into the fold,
caucus, or warren, or rebellious soul;
no crow is eagle there, no rabbit rat.
What are these talons in me clutching at?

Loss talons loss, as hunger talons cold.
This inching flight and hunt cast up the mind
in nightmare fractions. The sum is salvage, the whole
last gadding claw of horror undefined.

Which monster is the human, which God's scold?
You strike and stricken fall, in either rôle.

The Rape of Europa

This age it is the same, with less remembered.
The first was mounted by a foam-white bull;
others that came after were less sure
what beast bore God upon them fatally.
Always Europa is a doubting mother,
seeing the torn place struggle to be healed;
while what is born lies shameless in her lap.

This age her whole loveliness lies mauled,
battered and barren from a six years' bout,
so trod and torn, grossness itself defiled.
Though none could seem to mother her but earth
man monstered God upon her nonetheless.
The muck she lies in mocks the muck of birth,
and what is born lies blameless in her lap.

Horror got out of horror may yet be blest
when the great scar of birth begins to scab
and with each change of weather pull and burn
and the wound verge on flow. What bore, tore;
the horror and the glory are the same.
Man's hope the wound, God's memory the scar!
—else what is born lies nameless in her lap.

Ithyphallics

Surely we hear thunder
finding on this morning
all our substance wonder.

Wonder is self-guiding,
winds itself a wishwood
labyrinthine hiding.

Hiding is from ocean;
all around and under,
its dividing motion;
all inside, its thunder.

The Communiqués from Yalta

Not heart, not soul, and not their joined intent,
not these alone, but the whole process, breaking;
these are not salvo sounds, but fire raking
all hope, all memory, all undertaking.

—Who mocks the mockers when mockery is spent?
When will this dry tree I clutch be done shaking?

                      [Luke xxiii, 31]

PREVIOUSLY UNCOLLECTED POEMS

Dates of original publication, when known, have been added in brackets at the end of each poem

Autumn Sonata:
To John Marshall

i

I am a violin that fills
The solitude with strange and shifting melodies.
Whether the music sings of flowers, of trees,
Or of a range of grave-sown hills,
It leaps, and dies, and leaps again, afire.
Now a strolling fiddler, dressed as a buffoon,
Strikes up on me an airy tune;
Then another, face and garments ashen grey,
Stops my strings dead as he snatches me away;
But the third makes me tremble with desire.

I will build an Autumn shrine here by the river—
All her vague perfume is imprisoned here.
This is the harvest of the year;
Flowers that fade, and their beauty fresh forever,
She gathers here in barns, or throws away
There on her piles of chaff. . . .
Long grass grows thin and spare along the leas,
But endless are the dwarf birch-trees.
This unfrequented stretch today
Beneath the autumnal alchemy is half
Enchanted. Faint musicians play
The eternal rhythm for the birches' dance.
Light and shadow dart and glance
On their leafy undulating,
Color, motion gaily mating
As they ripple to and fro—
Ah! how delicately slow.
Why must I see them grimly dwarfed forevermore,
Stunted to children's growth when they are old and grey,
Bitter within, and twisted at the very core

Into a broken shape their Maker hurled away?
Yet, in their every contortion, grotesquely their heads
Yearn for the home of the stars, but with yearning that dreads
Hopeless conclusion to all of its skyward desires. . . .
Autumn still has spared the fires
Of some asters, bluer than dawn
When the last faint star is gone
And the sun is yet unseen.
They are alone; round them the withered goldenrod
Mocks in its blackness all the fleeting blue and green—
Has it been burned with the sorrow of forgotten God?
Look where the bulrushes wave; a scarce visible seed
Floats like a dream that strays lost through the dazzling day;
Chasing a song till the chase has grown into a need—
Fragile as man, with its goal nigh forgotten and gray. . . .
Back of me, a little rise,
Gemmed with many a gravestone, lies.
White burns out beneath the sun
Brilliant on a ground of dun
Mingled with a wild profusion
Of red, green, yellow, in confusion
Scattered madly here and there—
Glory that shouts through sunlit air.
And yet the leaves were made of corpses, that were stirred
To splendid life by sunlight—once more dead they lie.
No, not entirely; there on the crest of the hill,
Thwarted forever, a stern-outlined tower is still
Facing forever the riddle upon the sky's face. . . .
What have I heard—
Could it have been only that dun bird?
Nigh insanely merry, it is leaping over
Every solemn musical constraint;
It would make a jester of a heartsick lover—
An inebriate of a saint.

ii

So ardently the late song-sparrow chortles there
That he is heedless of the penetrating air;
The trees of that steep hillslope are his song—
One slim and trembling, but the other strong;
"See those two trees, linked hand in hand;
Slender the one, trembling and bending
Forward to see where she can stand
When she steps downward warily.
Mighty her lord—mighty the laughter
Which with his shoulders back he is sending
Over the pools of the aster sea.
This is their honeymoon; suddenly
She was caught up in a young desire
To wade in the flowers, repenting it after
Feeling the cold caress of the pool.
Loudly he mocks her—'Dear little fool;
Foolish your longing, foolish your fright';
Loudly he mocks, but that very fire
Comes from his heart, which love keeps alight."
Nor the bird, his song is no delightful jest,
But eager to find a home in that slim tree
He darts into her warm young breast;—
Behind, a tombstone looms up sombrely.

iii

To know that grave, I do not have to read
The stone. Sunlight that dances on the air,
White arms that glisten as they row—the seed
Of all our mortal joy lies stifled there.
Safe in his nest, the sparrow's song is done;
Sleep and warm feathers carrying off his care,
He dreams of summer laughing in the sun.
But in the chill we dream of Winter's might
Lopping the flowers' heads off one by one.

Go to the graveyard sorrowing, for night
And pain are living now; the dwindling day
Dies swiftly to obscure and trembling light.
All her bright merriment had passed away
Into profound unrestfulness, and I
Am overflowing, shaking tense and grey
With all desire. Do not ask me why;
Ask the young moon slow gliding up the sky.

iv

The moon—passionless mother of that double passion
Fated to swell in man, fated to die:
For love, whose mighty fires are ashen
When the moon has left the sky
Whence she had lighted them an hour before;
And for the sea, where tides that rule the shore,
At the moon's behest retire brokenly. . . .
The moon creates in me a yearning greater than me
(Land-locked, unloved, unloving) for love and for the sea.
I must escape, and not look at the sky,
But, lest the goddess should consume me, I
In the chill air will shiver,
Gazing the hill, and listening to the river. . . .
A late launch passes quickly, mystery
Born furtive in the night;
Low-glimmering waves surge rapidly.
Have you felt the might
Of all man's old desire for the sea? . . .
Lightlier still
Than the water lapped the smooth, wet shore,
Two lovers murmur on the hill;
They wrap the world in their embrace—
Do you feel the ancient longing for a perfect face? . . .
All is desire, desire I cannot quench
How it has seized me, nor could I escape before.

I would run up the sudden graveyard slope;
Among the graves would neither halt nor blench,
But to the tower I would grope,
Spring swiftly up the stairs, break down the bars,
And on the turret overhead
Wildly would fling my arms up from the dead,
Exultant and desirous, at the stars.

A Testament on Faith

But come now, it is like this
This is the way we touch and hinge
and brush and overlap:
it is the way that our lives fall together, cringe
together, and fall, and fall apart;—
the fresh bulk of a largest wave runs slap
against us, and we are free of earth;
borne shoreward in the wave,
borne shoreward resting together
on a great pillow of waters
till the hard shore stops us
and the surf is flattened out
in thin transparent lace.

But come; if you but listen and let
my words reveal themselves
unscarred by questing interruption,
then maybe you will see and will not ask
again why anguish mars my face
before and after each and every kiss
you press upon me in your great dream of grace.
Ah, listen!
It is like this.
You must not ask.
You must not question, only listen.

(And all the while I speak
I watch, I look, I see your eyelids glisten
dropping tiny prophecies.
I think if I kept still I should know
all that deepest knowledge that your silence holds
a great and brimming bowl
precarious before me.
And yet I speak.)

But listen.
You must not ask.
(This torture makes you look too droll.)
But listen.
It is like this.
I tell the whole.

The first touch when our first darkness fell, a mask
forever glued upon us,
signed certainly a terrible eruption,
marked certainly as onus
a sort of endless war for peace.
It is as if my body struggled ever,
ever upwards under sea,
and a heavy current bore me down.
Because I cannot wait until I drown
I struggle upward, and often,
in a dream a moment wraps me in,
feel almost free,
feel almost in the air.

It is like that.
We are together in our need,
and we float together.
Yet when the whirlpool whirls and sucks our feet
and overwhelms our strength again
and pulls our struggling bodies down, our greed
for life—or maybe sudden jealousy—
will make me clutch your hair,
will make you snatch my throat
between your murderous hands,
so that we drown.

Ah, do we clasp ourselves
to gain a union?
or do we wrestle?

I have seen your lips curl back
and gape around a frothing mouth,
and I have seen likewise a murderess,
with face like yours, go black.
Then we are bloody, suffering communion—
we who have dreamed that we were elves,
children of our fathers' gods
wandering in misted woodland alleys
shedding perfumes as we went.
Memories; blood stains, clotted wounds.
Shrines; tombs of the slain gods.

It is impossible to trust another's love,
and I would rather listen while your silence falls
a level rain among the air I breathe,
I would rather teach you chess
and see your drollest eyes confess
delicious bewilderment.
And yet I speak.
I do not trust.

The god lives never where the heart demands,
the god lives never in the clasping hands,
or lives there only as a pressure pressed
by him who loves.
Yet now I talk to you
and trust you hear my words, and trust you know
your force is sharp in all my actions.
I must explain. It is like this.
It's not my lips and hands,
it is my lips against your lips, my hands
fumbling among your hands,
it's what of me you make your own
that you desire.
And how can this thing last?

You think I bite my nose off,
spoil my face
for nothing.
But think.
When you have used me,
sucked me dry,
and thrown me out
to fertilize some other's field
with fervour of the second rate,
with passion most adulterate,
with mask turned inside out—
for how can this thing last?—
think then what kind of brittle shell I'll be.
For how can this thing last?
And when it's passed,
then how shall I forget the tremors,
the tremors and the terrors which passed
here between us,
which passed
as irrevocable as any history
of love and war?

                It is impossible to trust,
impossible to swear by anyone at all.

But I am tempted; I do not go.
It is like this:
I remember breezes meet and build a wind to blow
about the world.
Likewise all the trifling words we drop
so carelessly from time to time,
all the broken sentences that each of us
has finished for the other,
all the shrinkings and the greetings
we have suffered time and time again,
and all the thousand hopes we did not dare discuss—
in short, all we have felt in space and time

accumulates and forms one wind
thick against our nostrils,
forms the echo of our lives,
records our history.

And yet each ply of wind,
each volume of the air I deem I breathe,
is fugitive and is not breathed again,
so I can never swear I breathed at all.
It is impossible to trust,
impossible to swear by anything at all.
There are so many winds and tides, both high and low,
so great a multitude of winds and waters flow—
that of which one of them it is the rise and fall
which I forever treasure—that I cannot say.
I know surely, deeply, as I know dusk droops,
only a tangle of contacts among some shadow,
among penumbra cast by you and me,
the small, soft things of a life.

Once two people talked;
now two others think of them who passed
when their first darkness fell, a mask
forever glued upon them;
now two others grieve.

Can we, thought-weary of them who fell,
go on, and on, among the troubled rumours of their lives?

Words, words—and do you take them?
Words, sounds, the hard ruse of truth,
the bitter wind of deceit.
A sick heart babbles,
babbles and crumbles with old ills.
Words, words—and do you take them?

The words harry,
the words harry, snarl like broken gods—
the fallen deities of our sunken past.
And yet I speak them.
The words harry,
the words strain, scurry, belch, spew;
charged with meaning they can never carry
pour put of my mouth perpetual vomit.
And yet I speak them.

But come now and listen,
and is it not like this?

I stand here talking,
shaping preposterous figures for our lives;
I stand here talking,
watching the grave sorrow of your loveliness
bend down silent before me,
charging my body deeper with your silence
than my words can ever charge you with their noise.

It is like this.
In these short days you have grown old
within me,
grown old and steadfast
like everything that time has left behind.
It is like this.

I do not speak any more, because my mind,
in all its emptiness,
is somehow fuller than I have ever known it.

I do not trust; and yet I do not go.

The words harry,
and leave my life behind,
almost lifeless among our past,
among the contacts of the shadows you have cast
upon it.

Mr. Virtue and the Three Bears

> We hammer out tunes to make bears
> dance when we long to move the stars.
> —Flaubert

> This morning at his gas stand outside
> Lucerne on Route 1, Mr. Virtue was found
> devoured by his bear. Mr. Virtue left no known
> relatives.—Remembered from Bangor *Daily News*

I knew a bear once ate a man named Virtue
All but a mire of clothes, an unlicked bear
Caught, a May cub, to dance for soda pop;
Who when half-grown lumbered before us slowly,
Gurgling and belching in the gas-stand yard,
On a sorry chain, and made rough music there.

A chattel property of Mr. Virtue,
Untaxable and nameless, this black bear,
For some a joke to sell flat soda pop,
For some terror in chains, wove himself slowly
Through foundered postures, till hunger smalled his yard,
And he broke free by eating Virtue there.

If no kin came to claim the clothes of Virtue,
Yet hundreds claimed themselves in that black bear
And drank the upset crate of soda pop,
Kin drinking kin: drinking the stink that slowly,
Like a bear's pavanne, swept the gravel yard
And made of vertigo a music there.

So fell the single hymn to Mr. Virtue:
In rough music that burst from that young bear
When sudden soda in his loins went pop,
All longing and no hope, and he danced slowly,
Rearing and dropping in his chain-swept yard,
Till Mr. Virtue dumped spoiled blueberries there.

—And yet, there move two musics wooing Virtue:
Those of the Great and of the Lesser Bear,
Of the star falling and of new soda pop;
And these two bears dance best when long time slowly,
Overhead, the Dipper spills by inch and yard
The Northern Lights on us from darkness there.

So praises blew in this bear-feast on Virtue.
The greater sprang within the lesser bear
In music wild in the spilled light, to pop,
And by created hunger move, most slowly,
The blacker stars, fast-set in their hard yard,
To loose their everlasting shivers there.

Let us in virtue so beseech the bear,
With soda pop, that he may dancing slowly
Move in our yard constellations darkly there.

Alma Venus

The old old men, since they have wit
To count no thing entirely done,
No race completely run,
Will pardon me that I should sit
Beating my days out in the sun;
That I should never lift a finger,
Nor urge one thought ahead,
Except maybe to linger
Upon some image that might else have fled,
A wind-borne shaft of dust to join the dead.
They'll pardon me that I should choose,
For all my laziness,
Out of the images
That contemplative men may use
To dramatize their reveries,
That of a noble woman in her ease.
No man's that old and anxious after death
But that old memories will flood
With new-born sweetness all his blood
If this grave woman cool him with her breath,
Or drop her hair on him, a perfumed hood.

The old old men will pardon me
That I have, breathing in my mind
And stretched like flesh upon my nerves,
The one life older than all history,
Older than any dust they find
Cluttering Egypt's infancy
Or Greece's full age, or Rome declined,
The oldest goddess that an old man serves.

Looking at her there where she lies
I see, for all the time she's run,
There's not that beauty in her eyes
A common woman might have earned
Out of such seasons in love's school;
Nor yet that look of cool
Extravagant indifference
A lesser spirit might have learned
When so much adulation had been won
And with so little violence.
I think (maybe because of the intense
Heat of the ancient sun)
That she has whirled too many an identical round
Of bitter spring and swollen June
Ever to be completely beautiful
Or perfect like those women snared in dreams.
Looking at her grave nakedness it seems
Her flesh has been long trodden, like that ground
Where the world's playboy and the world's fool,
Where Socrates and Hercules
Tramped smooth the narrow pound.
So if the old old men forgive me
I'll say she is more powerful
And far more wise
Than any Socrates and Hercules.
I think maybe there stir
In her most muscular broad thighs
All men that ever were.

[1926]

Last Things

Now what I want
Out of these days is one
Still hour time shall not taunt
Me with the beautiful things undone
Or bitterly incomplete;
I would meet
Between the midnight and the first succeeding bell
One hour brimful as the sea,
One body deep as my breath in me:
So I would do my last things well.

[1927]

Effigy

i

I saw a boy, once, put a thinking hand
across eternity (the pasture bars)
slowly, and touch, almost, the horse's nose;
and the horse baulk, then nuzzle patiently.
So I would enter a friend's house. So I,
each in its time, would enter love, would die.

ii

The man looked up as the sun went down and I said
   Brother
behold the passing of our context, the wind
shrinks from the felicity of night, the small
white flowers between the pebbles are less white;
the odour of pennyroyal, where your fingers
frittered and bruised the fresh leaves, is less
pungent. Behold we are absent from our love, we are
lost to the common undertaking of our lives; there are
unleashed within us the small animals of silence
and these keep watch between us.—Neither my brother
nor I nor the brown air which protected us
could ever give heed one to the other.

iii

I looked at him who had that day been with me
digging for death, and so was set apart
so long his eyes took on that tarnished look
that all eyes too much looked in wear, and thought:
that tarnish must be what he sees in me;
else we are mirrors . . . Afterwards I said,
This is a silence we have dug here, not
a death. Silence is the more interminable.

iv

Three years ago that man whom I
Imagined imperturbable,
The dream of courtesy,
Blew up most suddenly
That he with a great splurge of blood might die
And find one sleep insensible.

The man grew cruel in his mind
And sacked the fastness of his soul,
That out of violence
Death's hushing excellence
Might fall and leave him cold and disciplined
Beyond debate, above control.

Three years in death. Now I have learned
What mockery our love appeared
When all our thoughtless care
Took an imagined share
In that untroubled mask of life he spurned
And sometimes in his wisdom feared.
Should I make him an effigy
I'd choose a windy hillside place
And see his figure stand,
Giant upon the land,
A man most anxious for eternity
Lifting an awkward, naked face.

[1929]

Three Poems

Water-Ruined

Take, from these waters, Lord, their slowing,
Ah, take away, for me, their growing
Into a silence, their sheathing me.
In such stillness I can hardly be
More than a memory flowing
(Water-ruined) interminably.

Flower and Weed

Lacking another thought
Take rosemary I said
of the salt marsh kind
to bring those shortly dead
back from the damp lot
and cramp them in your mind:

and take the fireweed then I cried
that flames where a house once burned
for all those thoughts that never earned
by dignity of sense a peaceful death
and so have never died—
let them discomfort you and slack your breath.

This flower and this weed
shall sum us till we're dead indeed.

Of a Muchness

Sweet the cold sea-moss, the old
tide-sounds and sea-change, the folding
of the waters on the earth—sweet
the sea pools and enchanted

these to the salt verge of youth
the breaking of life upon the shore

and here the tree
that other sweetness
—look where the two thieves
their bright harsh eyes embrace
with all the slow variety
of Noah's Ark
male and female, each in kind.
Sweet are we
hanging taut on the like tree
of the great dark

—what mercy of this world
what roman spear
could sweeten so
the new year

[1930]

Ides of March to April Fool's

i

Although the rain had fallen many days
and the sun beat between times, snow still clung
stubborn along the northern slopes. I thought:
Here shall a man sit down and fortify
against the summer the weakness of his heart.
There was old ice upon the pond below
and older ice within me when I looked,
and doubted somehow that he breathed at all:
queried, there is no faith in simple things.

He paused, and humus dampened on his hands,
the itch of growing and insensitive things
fastened upon his fascinated palms
like the red needles of the ivy itch.
These are intercalary days, he said,
put in between the dead and living, bruised
and forfeited, to keep the calendar.
The second hand upon his watch was small
and itched relentlessly, but not, he thought,
more than the ultimate relenting hour;—
My watch is visible vicar to my heart,
measures its waiting as if waiting ended.

No wonder he went out. No wonder, too,
when he came home, he itched the more. The dead
were getting out of hand, the living lost.
Easter took wing, last year's forsythia
neared bloom, and sudden cats rode male the female
tattering agony at midnight with their
discovery. Lapis revolutus est,
moved from the dead, set on the living chest.
In short, he heard that so and so announced

themselves engaged and meant to propagate.
So flesh was turned to water turning flesh.

He questioned that. His honest eyes grew sore.
Escape or balm or waste, there was the low
last luxury of self-pollution—in flesh
sensual, or ascetic in the mind:—
escape the cap of emptiness, balm
in easy loss, in incompletion waste.
He took these thoughts and turned to water, turned
to the warm porcelain of a sleepy tub;
the body was a poor thing in a tub,
afterwards—toweled, rubbed, and crisp in cloth—
it seemed the poverty was left behind.

The grass was dead. The birds were travelers.
In springtime all things come before their time.

The man I thought of argued in the rain,
soliloquised in sunlight, dreamt in wind,
and inconsolable went home by twilight.
What if the whiskers thickened on his chin—
surely it was no more to say than this:
hibernal interludes were not for him
but winter-words, the stubble of the snow
(and thereby thus for me who thought of him).
No crocuses burst out among his hair.

He watched the razor bare the stringent skin
and then the small shorn hair run down the drain.

All winter long I stand here so, and grow.
I should have been winter-dead; at rest;
as numb, as dreamless, as the bears and bees,
quiescent, lost, at least, in earthy sleep,—
quickened with no unnecessary breath

and altogether hidden in the cold.
But no. I have been winter-stoked. I have
with vain-burning embraced the ice and snow.

Because I have had no quiet from the clock
nor any hour blotted completely out,
in springtime I am come before my time.

ii

The rain turned warmer with the days and thinned—
shower to drizzle, mist to simple air.
That is the equinox, a thinning rain.
The man I thought of thought and spared no thought
lest sparing one he should have lost all thought
and faced himself, without a thought, at loss
before the catechumen which is spring.
He queried breath, and sneezed, and breathed again
(this was his catechism one long day)
that breathing he breathed rain into his lungs
He thought: the pond will have no ice in it;
and went to see. Already there were flies
riffling and netting its windless end. He wept,
not in his eyes nor salt, but in his heart
and saltless gall, that neither he could keep
himself a statue, silent upon his years,
nor share the aimless miracle that brought
these faultless flies, without the flair of fate,
so briefly to their fate, then them replaced.

In me, he cried, nothing can be replaced.

East wind, he swore seawind, winged on the water,
bright fish leapt not to flies that were not there,—
but he flowed down in tidal heart to sea
that was not, maybe, but his hidden heart.
Great grey acres of glass beset him, stole

out of his heart its magic, when he turned,
imaged the whelm and roll of open sea.
These are greenhouses twice and thrice he said,
greenhouses, prisons to green growing things,
greenhouses, housing a fictive, steaming spring.

He thought, this simulacrum thought and prayed:
the sea herself is honest past belief;
I will go down and be undone by her,
undone beyond belief and passing faith.
But he was wrong. That day the sea was large,
swollen into a gale; too large for him
and his small thoughts. A smaller self turned back,
aching and twisting, a thought about to burst,
turned back for warmth and seed and earth—for all
the greenhouse life that lived in him—and did
adultery with summer in his heart.

[1931]

Night Piece

After a day of burrowing
among the living world's damp loam
some frail, sweetest imagined thing,
some memory has brought him home.

You will have seen him sit there reading
of Stephen Dedælus and Bloom,
his nerves excited, faintly bleeding,
as the words' ghosts ascend the gloom.

—Consider how the world goes blind
when finally he shuts his book
and gives the woman in his mind
one devastating final look.

Love of the body twists the heart,
the body swells with the soul's smart;
love is at first a summer ache,
but next the members burn with plague.

The web of kisses on the flesh
becomes in time a heavy mesh
that checkers the muscles of the soul
as those hard muscles stretch and roll.

—Hung on the blanket of the air
from firmest chin to faintest hair—
a lifetime in her face he stared,
lost all the moments they had shared.

[1931]

Less Love Than Eachness

Less love
than eachness clinging to the sill of sense,
less unity than choice:
tight finger to finger
eye to grave eye,
this perpetual greeting
the tide-rip at the meeting
of the tide and stream.

And so I asked little at first
of the beauty I had chosen;
prayers are not granted
them that ask but them that thirst
though all the estuary of the mind
flow up with hot salt springs
and blind.

Now in the dark of time
so much grows in me through the ground
is drinking me and drunken,
given and being given shrunken,
I cannot render
the final spasm of surrender,
but with the world go round and round,
eternal tide-rip of our greeting,
lubricious slime.

[1932]

Resurrection

I did not see the frigate Constitution,
her yards cock-billed and bare as if she still
lay unretrieved and rotting at her pier,
towed all the summer port to port,
a lubber's sport
to every ignorant patrioteer.

She should have had the same sea-burial
my great-grandfathers had that fought on her;
the inconsolable sea closing above her
with no sound but the scream of skittering gulls
and the wind dying where her sails had been.

Instead there are a thousand in her shrouds
swarming to set the sails that are not there.

[1932]

The Bull

There is a shaking of the chain
as the black mountain turns
rippling with fury and seed-pain
and all that muscle all that weight
rises and visibly burns
until he mount and meet
the anguish and faith of the heifer's heat
and she from precipitous lightning learns
her virgin fate.

As the head strains with dull, lost eye
and half-choking there escapes
the thick rale, the throttled sigh,
the sudden thunder claps
announcing the hot spurt gone home
and the stilled spasm in the womb.

Then if the great neck sag
a slaked moment and he paw the raw ground
there is Europa shrieking in my loins,
her weakness and her terror bound
by the torment the craving the greed
for the hot thunder-seed
already troubling the limp bag
under his groin.

[1934]

By Definition

Prudence is enervate hope
and hope one instinct or another soiled
with use, the smudge of bad art,
drudge of a broken heart:
does all the work when the will is spoiled.
I mean, by will, that consciousness of clean intent,
that tendency to move and know,
to realise in word and image obdurate things
to which the soul must needs consent:
thus wilful imagination willed the angel's wings.
That harridan who scrubs the floors—
do you wonder that she shrieks and means to kill?
She had a bad start; they taught her all the hopes
that keep her going beat with angels' wings.
As those who hear the midnight death-tick know,
nothing maddens like a yearned-for noise.
You, Prudence, are more literate and better dressed.
You think your heart is whole or else absorbed
by saving contract. Your art is more confused
than bad, more weak than mad, and hence you're bored.—
You think because your hope has gone to seed?
It is your clothes that hamper. I love you best
when wilful imagination wills you naked.
Consider, the gods whose will you nearly do
are merely mankind imaged in the nude.
The writing hand, by will, is naked too.

[1935]

On Excited Knees

My hands have clutched through woodmoss damp
 leaf-mould,
have curled to breaking on a splitting oar,
but neither got my hands with child; they fold
symbol and image in imperfect score.
But ever, still (I on excited knees),
the harrowed land awaits the greening rain,
new-found Atlantis looms through easing seas,
before my haunted hands unfold again.

It is imagination goes to seed
in me, dies as it must, like God or corn,
to prove the moment of its greatest need
lies in the death that after we most mourn.
 Why should I speak if all I value most
 bears the unreal terror, a spoken ghost?

[1938]

Half-Tide Ledge

Sunday the sea made morning worship, sang
Venite, Kyrie, and a long Amen,
over a flowing cassock did put on
glittering blindness, surplice of the sun.
Towards high noon her eldest, high-run tide
rebelled at formal song and in the Sanctus
made heavy mockery of God,
and I, almost before I knew it, saw
the altar ledges of the Lord awash.
These are the obsequies I think on most.

[1944]

All's the Foul Fiend's

Now in the fond unhappiness of sleep,
Again in that fonder dark, the waiting chair,
Time upon time, there mounts through my own deep
Honey of agony to tongueless prayer.

Both forearms ache, then lift and circling woo
(A yearn of fondest flesh) towards vivid stone
Waist to close knees. I am Pygmalion, I too,
And uncreate with what I would atone.

O viewless face, unseen O rose and wine,
O torso spoiled, plunder of damaged will,
All fades in my embrace: the sweet too fine
For flesh turns stone: the wraith of unused skill.

—These, alas these limbs I woo, infatuate
And constant, till the fiend fouls me and I create.

[1950]

Nigger Jim
(*For STC and Huck Finn*)

Coleridge found midnight creative frost,
inaccessible the keepsake of what is lost.

His the private century of laudanum,
the dark angel rubbing the heart-skin like a drum
with palm-heel stroke and finger-tip tap;
and the darker angel with hands like a waiting lap.

So midnight holds. At dawn frost makes, and breaks.
Huck Finn found pinnacles splintering,
apex mentis at raking dark,
synderesis scintilla, treasure of spark,
found conscience bigger than the self: when frost slakes
all that had been kept for wintering.

Midnight holds. Dawn breaks. Nigger Jim is skun;
now all that bog of indolence asteam in sun.

[1950]

And No Amends

Because you, like another, have demanded
   flesh in the ghost, hope in the host;
although you, like one other, are beach-stranded,
   and anhungered and lost,
in unappeasable need,
   oh, die not in this place
of most you I have made.

   There are no idols here, no hope delayed,
only longing and grace.
   Even these are uncopeable friends,
they devour their old selves:
   self-defeating and self-repeating,
the self toasting self, in longing, in grace:
   and no amends.

Oh, die not in this place.
   Here diminishes only,
with unspeakable longing,
   unbeseechable grace.

[1950]

Threnos

Among the grave, the gross, the green
everlasting images are seen:
the grace of God, old girls, and March grass
How hoarse in counterpart this theme,
an allelulia also alas.

See there upon full sea the still
Blossoming of Jordan's heath,
And on the change, all living ill:
O eddying, bodiless faith.

[1960]

Acknowledgments

Acknowledgment is made to the following magazines for certain poems included in this book:

In *From Jordan's Delight*: POETRY, THE AMERICAN MERCURY, HOUND AND HORN, THE MAGAZINE, THE SOUTHERN REVIEW, THE MONARCHIST QUARTERLY (formerly ANATHEMA), THE VIRGINIA QUARTERLY, THE NEW REPUBLIC, ALCESTIS, SMOKE

In *The Second World*: THE NATION, TWENTIETH CENTURY VERSE, THE KENYON REVIEW

In *The Good European*: PARTISAN REVIEW, THE SEWANEE REVIEW, CHIMERA, THE KENYON REVIEW

In *Previously Uncollected Poems*: POETRY, LARUS, HOUND AND HORN, PAGANY, MOSAIC, THE MAGAZINE, TWENTIETH CENTURY VERSE, PARTISAN REVIEW. Also, to A COMPREHENSIVE ANTHOLOGY OF AMERICAN POETRY, ed. Conrad Aiken (New York, 1929), and the YALE SERIES OF RECORDED POETRY (New Haven, 1960).

Library of Congress Cataloging in Publication Data
Blackmur, Richard P.   1904-1965.
   Poems.

PS3503.I266A17 1977   811'.5'2   76-39598
ISBN 0-691-06335-4
ISBN 0-691-01337-3 pbk.

LIBRARY OF DAVIDSON COLLEGE

Books on regular loan may be checked out for **two weeks**. Books must be presented at the Circulation Desk in order to be renewed.

A fine is charged after date due.

Special books are subject to special regulations at the discretion of the library staff.